REFLECTIONS ON
THE FRENCH REVOLUTION

A HILLSDALE SYMPOSIUM

REFLECTIONS ON THE FRENCH REVOLUTION

A HILLSDALE SYMPOSIUM

Edited by Stephen J. Tonsor

REGNERY GATEWAY
Washington, D.C.

Library of Congress Cataloging-in-Publication Data

Reflections on the French revolution : a Hillsdale symposium / edited
by Stephen J. Tonsor.
    p.   cm.
    "Originally presented in a February 1989 conference sponsored by
Hillsdale College's Center for Constructive Alternatives"—Introd.
    Includes bibliographical references.
    ISBN 0-89526-750-0
    1. France—History—Revolution, 1789–1799—Influence—
Congresses. 2. France—History—Revolution, 1789–1799—
Historiography—Congresses. 3. Revolutions—Public opinion—
History—Congresses.
I. Hillsdale College.   Center for Constructive Alternatives.
DC148.R44 1990
944.04—dc20   89-77161
                                               CIP

Published in the United States by
Regnery Gateway
1130 17th Street, NW
Washington, DC 20036

Distributed to the trade by
National Book Network
4720-A Boston Way
Lanham, MD 20706

Printed on acid free paper.
Manufactured in the United States of America.

10 9 8 7 6 5 4 3 2 1

ACKNOWLEDGMENTS

I SHOULD LIKE TO thank Hillsdale College for making this volume possible and especially to thank Thomas H. Conner and Kendall W. Brown for their invaluable assistance in helping to assemble this work. I should also like to thank Lissa Roche, of Hillsdale College, and Harry Crocker, of Regnery Gateway, for their editorial work, and Jennifer Reist, of Regnery Gateway, who guided the manuscript through to its completion.

CONTENTS

CONTENTS

ILLUSTRATIONS

FOREWORD

For the past century revolutions have been in vogue. To be revolutionary was to demonstrate one's modernity. College catalogues are filled with courses introduced by the word "revolution." Perhaps the discrediting of traditional European society caused by the folly of the First World War and the Russian Revolution of 1917 contributed to the renewed popularity of revolution after the failed revolutions of the nineteenth century. Certainly Marxism as a theoretical explanation of revolutionary history played a leading role in explaining and popularizing the French Revolution. The Marxist historians invented what Francois Furet has described as the "revolutionary catechism" which has dominated the study of the French Revolution and French history for fifty years.

But Marxism is in trouble. The Russian Revolution, which was its incarnation, has sickened, and Soviet Communism now appears to be in its death agony. Marxism, "the God that failed," unable to predict the future, no longer seems a safe interpretive guide to the past. Suddenly, the interpretation of the French Revolution that dominated the 1930s, 1940s, and 1950s is challenged, and in retreat, everywhere.

A new interpretation of the French Revolution appears to be blossoming into one of the most important revisionist historical efforts of our time. This "new" interpretation is essentially that of Edmund Burke, Thomas Carlyle, Alexis de Tocqueville, Hyppolite Taine, and Augustin Cochin, all of whom argued aspects of the "new" interpretation in the nineteenth and twentieth centuries.

The current debate between those suspicious of the French Revolution and those still eager to praise it is much alive in these lectures presented at Hillsdale College. This lecture series is remarkable and intensely interesting because it reveals the effort of a small college to engage with and think about one of the key events in the creation of modernity.

University of Michigan   Stephen J. Tonsor
Spring, 1990

INTRODUCTION

WHEN BRITISH HISTORIAN Paul Johnson sought to illuminate the intellectual motivation behind the American
Revolution and the U.S. Constitution, he looked to "the
comparatively new stress on equality and human rights
generated by French writers of the Enlightenment: Rousseau, Diderot and the other Encyclopaedists." When
Fortune memorialized what it called, "U.S.A.: The Permanent Revolution," most of its features began with ref-
erences to France. Why, after two hundred years, is the
French Revolution still with us? From nineteenth-
century Romantic poets to contemporary Marxist revisionist historians, the echoes of 1789 are still heard.

That the French Revolution has enduring significance
for France, and for all nations, is undeniable. What is less
certain, however, is how we are to interpret its legacy. Was
the French Revolution a victory of liberty over tyranny?
Was it an affirmation of human rights, or an ominous extension of the centralized state? Did it represent the triumph of the bourgeoisie in Marx's ongoing class struggle?

From the outset, observers were bound to compare the
French Revolution with the American revolutionary experience in 1776. It has been argued that both were part of
a broader process of democratic revolution in the West,
but many claim that the two were radically different in
character as well as outcome. The British statesman Edmund Burke joined American President John Adams in
deploring the "Terror" in France, while Adams' successor,
Thomas Jefferson, vowed that the fruits of democracy
would outweigh any excesses in the formation of the new
French republic. Did the ideals and the realities of 1776

and 1789 diverge? Alexis de Tocqueville, the French nobleman and writer, was able to capture, perhaps more percep-
tively than anyone else, the spirit of each and the impact
they would have upon the future. Both certainly inspired
many of the revolutions which have followed throughout
Europe, Latin America, and Asia.

The legacy of the French Revolution is still a subject of
heated debate. Of that legacy what ought we to commemorate in 1989? What should we celebrate? What should we
lament? Even the French are divided over this issue. With
the end of the *ancien régime* and the establishment of the
modern state, what was gained and what was lost, for
France and for the West?

The essays in this volume address such questions. Originally presented in a February 1989 conference sponsored
by Hillsdale College's Center for Constructive Alternatives, each one brings us closer to an understanding of the
unfulfilled promises of 1789.

Thomas H. Conner's "The Riddle of Revolution" gives a
chronological overview of the major events of the French
Revolution, which was brought on, primarily, by a series
of political and economic crises that the monarchy was
unable or unwilling to handle. The "shipwreck" of the
ancien régime was not, contrary to popular opinion, the
result of a conspiracy by Enlightenment intellectuals, nor
was it a searing class conflict. Conner warns, however,
that the "French Revolution will always mean different
things to different people" and that too many simplistic
characterizations have already been heaped upon the
events of 1789.

In "The Gods of Revolution," John Willson argues that it
is indeed possible to define the character of a revolution
without being simplistic. He sees the French Revolution
primarily as a movement that placed the state above all
else. In a detailed account of the French Revolution's deliberate and systematic persecution of clerics and religious believers, Willson attempts to demonstrate that its

nature was fundamentally flawed, that it was quintessentially anti-religious, and that it was not just a "good revolution gone bad."

Edmund Burke scholar Peter J. Stanlis notes that the great Irish statesman reviled the French Revolution as a "rebellion against God." For Burke, Rousseau's doctrine of the natural goodness of man and subsequent abandonment of moral law was the evil root of the Revolution and invited "chaos, anarchy, violence, and all of the characteristics that came to prevail." In the new Republic of Virtue, the Jacobins decided the fate of their countrymen according to this doctrine, and those insufficiently committed to the Revolution went to the guillotine. But, Stanlis notes, Burke did not discount economic and political causes either; he warned as early as the 1760s that France's enormous national debt and weak leadership threatened the monarchy.

In "The Age of the Guillotine," Erik Ritter von Kuehnelt-Leddihn joins Willson and Stanlis in agreeing that the French Revolution was no mere reaction against a repressive monarchy. The political and economic disintegration of the *ancien régime* was overshadowed by a moral breakdown and a fanatical commitment to democracy which allowed demagogues like the Marquis de Sade to bring on violence. For Leddihn, the Terror represents the essence, not the excesses, of the French Revolution.

Sam Knecht gives us a different perspective on the French Revolution by commenting on the art of the era, especially the works of the immensely popular Jacques Louis David. He focuses first on the monarchy and how paintings like the *Oath of the Horatii*, which depicts three Romans swearing loyalty to the state, actually had the opposite effect on a public that was increasingly hostile to the government of Louis XVI. During the Revolution, art subordinated itself to the republican state by commemorating virtually every major event, including the beheading of the king and queen. With the meteoric rise of Napoleon, painters and sculptors found a new way to indulge their obsession for political and ideological symbolism.

Russell Kirk reveals in "The Armed Doctrine in Fiction" another view of the French Revolution. He cites Charles Dickens' classic *Tale of Two Cities,* Victor Hugo's *Ninety-Three,* and Joseph Conrad's *The Rover* as fiction which not only shows "the follies of ideological infatuation," but the wrenching character of revolution and how it invariably destroys the lives of ordinary men and women. Kirk speculates about each author's ambivalent attitude toward the French Revolution: Dickens, disgusted by the decadence of the aristocracy, but still certain that the zealotry of the Jacobins was the greater evil; Hugo, convinced that the individual must be sacrificed on the altar of democracy, but still admiring defiant acts of *noblesse oblige;* and Conrad, contemptuous of radical ideologues but aware that we cannot be rid of them without resorting to violence ourselves.

"Equality as a Factor in the American and French Revolutions," by Stephen J. Tonsor, draws a sharp distinction between the American and French Revolutions. The American Revolution, he states unequivocally, was not, in any sense, equalitarian. It was controlled by the elite and its objective was political equality for Americans within the traditional hierarchy of Anglo-American society. The common law of England was still binding and as many historians have pointed out, the American Revolution resembled more of an effort to preserve than to transform the status quo. By contrast, the French Revolution was not led exclusively or even primarily by elites. France went through a bitter, bloody upheaval that was very unlike the American struggle. The unrealizable goal of absolute equality, which gripped peasants and intellectuals alike and which truly inspired the French Revolution, was what made the Terror inevitable, according to Tonsor.

Richard M. Ebeling makes the case in "The Triumph of

Statism" that even if there were no other factors involved, government mismanagement of the economy would have inevitably led to the downfall of the French monarchy. Louis XVI had bankrupted the treasury, deficit spending was out of control, private property was nationalized, wage and price controls were strangling industry, and inflation threatened the monetary system with collapse. The Revolution did not, however, produce meaningful economic reform; the new government imitated the mistakes of the old and launched even more strenuous efforts to regulate private enterprise and impose the will of the state.

The concluding essay, "The French Revolution and Modernity," by Kendall W. Brown, cautions, like the opening essay by Thomas H. Conner, that the French Revolution will always be surrounded by controversy. For Brown, the French Revolution has borne for far too long blame for all the evils of modernity. He credits it, at least partially, with a positive legacy of liberty and progress for all mankind. He also rejects the contention of other authors in this volume that the French Revolution paved the way for the Russian Revolution. That, he claims, would be exaggerating its influence. Says Brown:

> The French Revolution was a gate through which the Western world passed into modernity. It was not the only passageway; neither did it represent a clean break with the past and a jump-start on modernity. But the Revolution took pre-existing conditions and ideas which had been developing, particularly since the mid-1700s, passed them through a cataclysm, and changed forever the way humanity saw society, religion, the state, and the nation.

CHRONOLOGY:
The French Revolution, 1789–1799

August 1788	Convocation of Estates-General announced by Louis XVI
February 1789	Publication of Sieyès' *What Is the Third Estate?*
May 5, 1789	Estates-General convene
June 17, 1789	Third Estate declares itself the National Assembly
June 20, 1789	Tennis Court Oath
July 14, 1789	Storming of the Bastille
July–August 1789	The Great Fear in the countryside
August 4, 1789	National Assembly abolishes feudal privileges
August 27, 1789	National Assembly issues Declaration of the Rights of Man
October 5, 1789	Parisian women march on Versailles and force royal family to return to Paris
November 1789	National Assembly confiscates church lands
July 1790	Civil Constitution of the Clergy establishes a national church; Louis XVI agrees to accept a constitutional monarchy
June 1791	Arrest of the royal family after its attempted escape from France
August 1791	Declaration of Pillnitz by Austria and Prussia
April 1792	France declares war on Austria

August 1792	Louis XVI taken prisoner by Parisians; "Second French Revolution"
September 1792	September Massacres; National Convention declares France a republic and abolishes monarchy
January 1793	Execution of Louis XVI
February 1793	France declares war on Britain and Holland; Provincial cities revolt
March 1793	National Convention struggle between Girondists and the Mountain; France declares war on Spain
April–June 1793	Jacobins gain control of the Committee of Public Safety and arrest Brissotin leaders
July 1793	Marat assassinated and Robespierre enters Committee of Public Safety
September 1793	Price controls established
October 1793	Marie Antoinette executed
1793–1794	Reign of Terror in Paris and the provinces
Spring 1794	French armies victorious on all fronts
July 1794	Execution of Robespierre; Thermidorian Reaction begins
1795–1799	The Directory
1795	End of economic controls and suppression of the *sansculottes*; Louis XVII dies in prison
1797	Napoleon defeats Austrian armies in Italy
1798	Austria, Great Britain, and Russia form the Second Coalition against France
1799	Napoleon overthrows the Directory and seizes power

REFLECTIONS ON
THE FRENCH REVOLUTION

A HILLSDALE SYMPOSIUM

THE RIDDLE
OF REVOLUTION

THOMAS H. CONNER

Thomas H. Conner joined the Hillsdale faculty's history department in 1983 and for a number of years served as director of admissions for the College. He has also taught history at North Carolina State University and the University of North Carolina at Chapel Hill. He received his Ph.D. from the latter institution in 1983, writing his dissertation on "Parliament and the Making of Foreign Policy: France Under the Third Republic, 1875–1914," which was later presented at the Annual Great Lakes History Conference. Dr. Conner's major research interests include French government and politics and European diplomacy.

It is entirely fitting that the world has focused on the legacy of the French Revolution in 1989, the bicentennial year of its beginning. One thing is certain, however: the French had a much easier time determining when to begin their celebration than when to end it. Many Frenchmen and non-Frenchmen alike would have us believe that this Revolution has never ended; it certainly did not end soon enough for some. It is useful to call to mind in this connection an article from *Fortune* magazine in 1951, which characterized the American Revolution as "a permanent revolution." The American experience, the editors of the magazine wrote in that year, amounts to "a permanent revolution in the affairs of men ... a revolution of the human individual against all forms of enslavement; against all forms of earthly power . . . that seek to govern man without consulting his individual will." Well, there is a new discussion of the French Revolution making its way to press in the United States entitled *The Permanent Revolution*, and the appraisal nearly forty years apart of the two great revolutions of the last quarter of the eighteenth century in exactly the same manner should tell us something about the lasting significance and enduring vitality of both as we begin our own examination of the younger of the two.

My comments here should properly be called "The Riddles of Revolution," for there are multiple enigmas in the story of this momentous event. I intend to present a sampling of them to you, along with a brief chronological overview of the first decade of the Revolutionary era so that we all share some background in common for the rest of the essays. But I almost feel obliged to lay a thick fog of confusion regarding just how there came to be a revolution in France in the first place, and what it has meant. It is only fair that we should all be confused about these matters, because the historical profession that has repeatedly disassembled and reassembled the events of 1789, and those that led to them and stemmed from them, seems as far from a consensus today on these fundamental questions, especially on the question of origins, as it has ever been. As William Doyle, a noted British scholar on the Revolution, has written recently in an excellent summary of the last fifty years of revolutionary historiography, *Origins of the French Revolution*, historians in that time have spent more effort tearing into each others' work than seeking common ground. Doyle concludes that "a new synthesis, however difficult, however imperfect, however tentative, is urgently required." It would be vain of me to aim at such a consensus—but, I do propose, as Riddle Number One: How are the origins of the French Revolution to be explained? Along the way, we will survey one or two alternatives.

The origins of the French Revolution, in my view, lay in a political crisis that broke against the backdrop of an economic crisis and resulted in a radical reordering of French politics and society. The confluence of these two crises was termed by one of my most exciting professors in graduate school, George V. Taylor, a "shipwreck." The beautiful thing about this way of looking at the Revolution's origins is that, on the one hand, it is free of any scent of historical determinism, which the Marxist interpretation has shot through it, and secondly, it is free of any scent of conspiracy, which is how some bewildered contemporaries and some historians came to understand the Revolution—as the product of some intellectual conspiracy hatched by *devotées* of the Enlightenment. Most scholars have found it easier to dismiss the latter thesis, so we will explore briefly the former as the principal alternative to the one I will offer myself.

The Marxists, of course, believe that the Revolution was caused by and chiefly benefited the capitalist class, or the bourgeoisie, which was determined to break the power of the feudal aristocracy or land-owning nobility. This land-owning class, the Marxist argument runs, was targeted for destruction by the bourgeoisie precisely because the aristocracy was blocking the path of the bourgeoisie to political power and social status that were commensurate with its expanding wealth. And, moreover, all this was fated to happen—pre-determined, in other words by that very dynamic of history that Marx thought he saw, and which he thought would culminate in the victory of the proletariat. Before the proletariat could triumph over the bourgeoisie, however, the bourgeoisie had to triumph over the feudal aristocracy, and this essential step occurred, the Marxists believe, with the French Revolution. This interpretation looks at the Revolution, then, as an event which was social and economic in origin, but which clearly had political consequences. Taylor and the non-Marxists, by contrast, see the Revolution as political in origin with major social and economic consequences. If the Revolution sprang mostly from political causes, then, what brought it on? In brief, a crisis in state finances.

The French monarchy faced mounting debts as the 1780s wore on. Much of the staggering accumulation of red ink at this time is to be explained by France's sponsorship of the American Revolutionary War after 1778. It is ironic, though not altogether paradoxical, that the French would put their own fiscal solvency at risk to support a revolution made on principles which were so antithetical to their own political and social order. France's existing regime rested on absolute monarchy and inequality of rights—and neither of these ideas found any favor with the American revolutionaries. Nor was the French leadership enamored of the philosophy of the Declaration of Independence. What sold King Louis XVI on helping the Americans was the prospect of wounding the British and, in the process, avenging a humiliating defeat France had suffered at England's hand a generation earlier in the Seven Years' War.

If the French tasted sweet revenge at Cornwallis' surrender, they tasted the sour fruit of fiscal insolvency for their efforts before the decade was out. By 1786, debt service charges alone ate up 50 percent of the annual expenditure, and the government continued to spend about 25 percent more than it took in. (If historical comparison is your thing, the U.S. government was close to spending 25 percent more than it was taking in on several occasions under President Reagan, but debt service charges in fiscal 1989 only amounted to 15 to 16 percent of federal expenditures.) According to William Doyle, the French minister of finance approached the King at the end of 1786 and said roughly the following: "We cannot go on like this. I cannot continue to cover our deficits with new borrowing because financiers are losing confidence. We can effect certain economies, but not enough to rescue us. We cannot repudiate the debt because that would utterly destroy our credit. We have got to come up with more revenue." Had Louis XVI been George Bush, he would have undoubtedly replied: "Read my lips. No new taxes!" Actually, the King was not opposed to new taxes, as we'll see, though this whole scene is eerily familiar, isn't it? Well, at this point, the plot thickens.

The revenue needed was undoubtedly there. France was not a poor country, though her government was obviously revenue poor. The greatest untapped pool of revenue was the nobility, which owned about 35 percent of the land in the country, while amounting to only two to three percent of the population, and was exempt from most forms of taxation. As the King's finance minister declared in frustration as this crisis was breaking, it was a case of "the richest class contributing least." To resolve this problem, the government proposed a series of reforms, the key provision of which was a tax on land that all landowners, even the privileged orders of nobility and clergy, would be required to pay. Early in 1787, the King invited 144 handpicked "notables," prominent people mostly from the privileged estates, to come to Versailles and discuss the proposed reforms.

The King thought he had chosen people who would see things his way and sanction the new laws. The meeting broke up, however, without their consenting to the most important parts of the government's program. The notables were not convinced new taxes were needed; indeed, the government's financial records were such a mess that nobody could really tell how much money there was. They contended, moreover, that if the King meant to enact reforms which fundamentally contradicted tradition, such as ending the tax exemption of the privileged orders, he needed to convoke the Estates-General. This was a body representing all three orders in French society (clergy, nobility, and commoners) which had not met since 1614, but which still stood as the last recourse for monarchs who wished to consult the nation in dire emergencies. The fact that this institution had been dormant for nearly two centuries indicates that, until the 1780s, French kings had wielded the absolute power they claimed more or less effectively. But, Louis XVI's financial troubles had shown that he was not doing that and, not surprisingly, other important components of the state, especially the nobility, sought to take advantage of his distress and gain a powerful voice in the affairs of state themselves. What was at issue in "the crisis of the pre-Revolution," then, was nothing less than how France was going to be governed. Absolute power in the hands of Louis XVI had brought the country to the brink of financial incapacitation. In the effort to resolve that crisis, powerful interests, beginning with the nobility, would seek permanently to curtail the prerogatives of the King.

Needless to say, Louis XVI did not make haste to call the Estates-General. From February 1787 until August 1788, he refused to do so and tried instead to implement his reform program, including the controversial land tax and an equally controversial stamp tax, by decree. Even though the French monarch theoretically possessed absolute power, he was obliged to have all his decrees registered by law courts known as *parlements*, which were populated by the nobility. Not surprisingly, the *parlements* repeatedly refused to comply with the King's wishes during this critical time, insisting that the only body competent to rule on such momentous issues was the Estates-General. Louis, in theory, had the power to decree laws over the objection of these courts, but by 1788, his opposition had become so vociferous and disruptive that he simply could not employ despotic means effectively. In August 1788, the King finally relented and called the Estates-General for the following May, but only after his finance minister reported to him that the treasury was literally empty.

The Old Regime monarchy, in the opinion of Doyle, ended in August 1788 because it was powerless to act on any important matter until the Estates-General convened. If this assessment is true, it is important to note that the destructive agent of the monarchy's power was certainly not the populace at large; rather, it was the nobility acting through the *parlements*. The first stage of the dismantling of the Old Regime, a process completed by the Revolution, was a revolt of the aristocracy aimed at limiting the powers of the King. (This interpretation is eloquently put forth by Georges Lefebvre, a Marxist historian, and a number of non-Marxists generally share this view.) It was this revolt which required the King to call the Estates-General, and once that body convened it became the battleground to determine which group would take the lead in regenerating the nation. Once it was determined who would control the Estates-General—this battle raged until late June—then attention could be turned to what would be done by way of reform. "The French Revolution," as Doyle has written, "was the process by which these matters worked themselves out."

The Estates-General did not last two months; it broke up over the question of how it would decide issues. Tradition held that this body would vote by order—that the clergy had one vote, the nobility had one vote, and the commoners one vote. What this meant was that the privileged orders together possessed the power to dictate all decisions. The Third Estate, whose representation had been doubled (to 600 men—the others had 300) as a concession by the King some time earlier, held out for "vote by head." With defections from reform-minded nobility and clergy, this procedure would have held out reasonable hope that constitutional reform might come without violent revolution. As it happened, the privileged orders would not compromise on this point, and in mid-June, the representatives of the Third Estate, claiming that they alone spoke for the interests of the whole nation, bolted from the Estates-General and constituted themselves as the National Assembly. To seal the irreversibility of this action, the men of the Third Estate on June 20 swore an oath on an indoor Tennis Court at Versailles (the famous "Tennis Court Oath") not to disband until they had written a constitution. Several days later, the King yielded to this act of defiance—and the French Revolution was underway. The revolt of the Third Estate against the traditional organization of the Estates-General, in other words, was the first truly revolutionary act.

The fact that the representation of the Third Estate in the Estates-General was comprised mostly of bourgeoisie—professionals, lawyers, wealthy men of commerce—has fuelled the Marxist contention that the establishment of the National Assembly constituted a revolution of the bourgeoisie against the traditional aristocracy. What gave unity to this revolt of the Third Estate was not the selfish, or self-conscious interest of a class defined by its relationship to the means of production; rather, what gave impetus to this event was a vision that France should be more than its privileged orders, that it should be everybody who lived within its borders. If almost everybody was in the Third Estate (and roughly 95 percent of the population was), then it stood to reason that the representatives of this order should speak for the entire nation. This had been the point of one of the best-known popular pamphlets to appear during the election campaigns for representatives to the Estates-General, the Abbé Sieyès's *What Is the Third Estate?*

"What is the Third Estate?" the author had asked.
"Everything."
"What has it been in the political order until now?"
"Nothing."
"What does it seek?"

"To become something."

By the end of June, it had become something. From this moment on, the reordering and regeneration of French society would be directed by the Third Estate.

Yet this victory seemed fragile at the end of June and into July. The King outwardly sanctioned the legitimacy of the National Assembly, but this blessing had come grudgingly. At the same time, royal troops began massing on the outskirts of the capital. Rumors spread that Louis was planning to move forcibly at some point to disband the Assembly. This uneasiness, compounded by profound economic hardship, led to the first mass popular stroke of the Revolution—the storming of the Bastille on July 14, 1789. The Bastille was a royal prison in the heart of Paris. It was a logical target for attack by the mob not only because it symbolized royal despotism, but because it stored weapons which the people of Paris could use to defend themselves against the feared counter-stroke by the King. The mob took the Bastille, the garrison there was butchered, the Revolution had gained a triumph that would echo through the ages, and France had acquired a date to commemorate as the birthday of its freedom.

I observed earlier that it was a political crisis intersecting with an economic crisis which produced the "shipwreck" of the Old Regime. Now we must assess briefly the impact of the prolonged economic crisis which shadowed and shaped the course of the Revolution. During the late 1780s, France became mired in a severe agricultural and industrial depression which caused mass unemployment, food shortages, and widespread hunger. This downturn had the effect of upsetting the masses just at the time when a high-stakes political contest was underway. The ordinary Frenchman, whom we may characterize as an illiterate peasant in the countryside or an illiterate worker in the city, could not have understood much of the political discourse aimed at settling constitutional matters. But he was led to believe that the Estates-General and, later, the National Assembly would bring him relief, and he was in a high state of excitement over that prospect. From this came an instinctive popular support for the Revolution which is brutally evident after July 1789. Mob actions, such as the storming of the Bastille and the "Great Fear" which was its counterpart in the countryside, introduced new pressures on the National Assembly to get on with the destruction of the Old Regime. If the opposition of the aristocracy to the King was one of the essential preconditions for the Revolution, and the bourgeoisie fathered the first revolutionary act, the masses in the cities and on the farm propelled this process down paths and at speeds scarcely predictable earlier on.

The events of August 4, 1789, illustrate this interaction of popular violence and constitutional reform. On this date, in what one historian, Leo Gershoy, has called "an indescribable and sustained [he might also have said spontaneous] movement of interested and disinterested self-sacrifice," the National Assembly, now a collection of mostly Third Estate deputies but also containing some nobles and clergy, ended the legal inequalities of the Old Regime. The nobility surrendered its tax exemptions, judicial rights over its tenants, and special hunting and fishing privileges; the clergy surrendered the tithe; and so it went. By the time this meeting was over, France had suddenly become a nation whose citizens enjoyed equal standing before the law—now to be uniform law in all parts of the country—and were eligible for all public offices. What explains the timing of the August 4th decrees is the peasant violence of the "Great Fear," which was directed against a host of feudal obligations and restrictions that had oppressed the rural masses since time immemorial. This violence convinced the lawmakers that the people needed relief from these burdens. What explains the actual solution? I think, the cold realization that fairness dictated it.

By the end of August, the essential principles of the

Revolution had found expression in the Declaration of the Rights of Man and of the Citizen, which became the preamble to the constitution of 1791, the first constitution of the new regime. This first effort at composing a revolutionary credo reveals that, by this point, the Revolution was affirming "in the presence and under the auspices of the Supreme Being" ("Enlightenmentese" for "God") that "men are born and remain free and equal in rights," that "the aim of all political association is the preservation of the natural and imprescriptable rights of man," that sovereign power resides "in the nation" (the sum total of all citizens), that property was "an inviolable and sacred right," and that every citizen may "speak, write, and print with freedom"—just to cite some of the provisions of this piece. In this Declaration, we find much common ground with the principles and ideals of the American Revolution. We also see much of the ideology and vocabulary of the Enlightenment. We see little that would seem explicitly menacing, though much that might be implicitly menacing depending on the ideological moorings of the beholder. Nonetheless, there is little in the Declaration that hinted at the brutal abuses of these very same rights that would occur before the Revolution had run its course. Indeed, if the Revolution had stopped here, most everyone might find it possible to celebrate it. So, we arrive at Riddle Number Two: Why didn't the Revolution stop here?

The process carried further because the National Constituent Assembly, as it was now called, had not yet completed shoring up the revolutionary regime or giving it institutional form. Toward that end, the Assembly proceeded next to attack the institutionalized Church, which had of course been one of the privileged estates of the Old Regime. In November 1789, the Assembly placed all Church lands at the disposal of the state in order to secure a new wave of government borrowing. Here we have additional fall-out from the fiscal crisis which provoked the

13

Revolution, but we also have something more: the beginning of a systematic effort by the Assembly to nationalize
the Church, to merge religious life with civic life, and to
subordinate the Church totally to the authority of the
state. The Civil Constitution of the Clergy, enacted in July
1790, actually made all clergy paid officials of the state
and provided that they be elected to their offices by the
same secular bodies that chose political functionaries.
Such measures seemed perfectly logical to the National
Assembly, which was determined to guarantee that all
components of the state pulled in the same direction. To
many, if not most sincere churchmen, this arrangement
smacked of hostility toward religion and stood as a gross
perversion of the status of the clergy. One thing can be said
with certainty: the religious laws of 1790, in the words of
Leo Gershoy, "did more than any single act of the Constituent Assembly to develop the counterrevolution." Other-
wise put, these laws pushed substantial numbers of
Frenchmen and whole regions of the country into outright
opposition to the Revolution. And, as counterrevolutionary sentiment intensified, the nation was doomed to more
violence and unforeseen twists and turns in the revolutionary path.

The National Constituent Assembly finished its work
in 1791 when the constitution it had written took effect.
The most important features of this constitution were
that the King remained head of state, but his powers were
limited; a unicameral Legislative Assembly elected by a
restricted franchise would pass all laws; administratively
France was completely reorganized into eighty-three
roughly comparable departments uniformly subject to the
central authority of the state; and, finally, the Church was
nationalized. In just two years, then, the Old Regime had
been torn down, pillar by pillar. The French could have
used nothing better at this point than a period of calm to
habituate themselves to the new order. Alas, this was
denied them.

Even before the new Legislative Assembly began to sit, the King tried to flee, with his family, to join counterrevolutionary elements outside of the country. Louis made it to within about twenty miles of the border before his carriage was halted at the little town of Varennes, and the whole pack of them was returned to Paris. The King would retain his office for more than a year after the flight to Varennes, but he was the object of strong suspicion that whole time and this incident intensified agitation for France to become a republic and to push the Revolution further. The ubiquitous mobs in Paris became more excitable, too, at the scent of counterrevolution in their midst and out of impatience at the refusal of economic conditions to improve. In August 1791, Austria and Prussia, two of the most powerful states in Europe, declared at Pillnitz their commitment to stamping out revolution in France. Opinion in the fractious Legislative Assembly divided over how to respond to this overt internationalization of the counterrevolution, but in April 1792, France declared war on Austria. To assess the motives of all the politicians, generals, ordinary people, and the King who participated in this decision would unduly burden us. Suffice it to say that the coming of war radicalized the Revolution—broadened it, deepened it, brutalized it, and arguably diverted it down paths it might never have taken had the country remained at peace with its neighbors.

This was so, at first, because the war went badly for France. Early reverses in the field prompted harsh attacks against the government. Spearheading these attacks were the Jacobins, a radical left-wing faction in the Assembly supported by clubs in many parts of the country. Their leader was a Parisian lawyer named Robespierre, and their agenda called for the overthrow of Louis XVI and the establishment of rule by all the people, not just the elite of former nobility and propertied commoners who voted and held office under the young constitution. Robespierre's egalitarian and republican views found special favor with the restless mobs in Paris, and on August 10, 1792, he was able to stir the crowds into an insurrection. The royal palace was invaded, the royal family fled and was eventually arrested, and the constitution of 1791 was scrapped. By the end of September 1792, Louis XVI had been formally deposed, and France was declared a republic. To dramatize this radical departure a new calendar was decreed, and time started afresh from September 22, the first day of the Year 1. France had experienced a second revolution, and the violence in which it was born would not quickly abate.

Violence at home continued, for one thing, because the news from the front remained bad. Just nine days after the King fell, Prussian troops breached the frontier and captured a major fortress town. In early September, Verdun seemed ready to fall, and with the loss of this vital point, the road to Paris would lay wide open. Parisians formed into volunteer units and made ready to head for the front. Before departing, however, many of them were overcome with foreboding. The prisons in the city were filled to overflowing with rebellious priests, suspected counter-revolutionaries, and the usual assortment of ordinary criminals. What might these dangerous characters do once the city was depleted of its fighting men? The fears thus generated touched off the so-called September massacres, a spontaneous orgy of violence which claimed the lives of more than 1,100 prisoners in Paris alone and which has done much to discredit this phase of the Revolution, for this sort of rampant killing would carry on for most of the next two years, climaxing in the Reign of Terror. The King himself was put on trial at the end of 1792 when damning new evidence of his counterrevolutionary activity surfaced. A vote of the National Convention sent Louis XVI to the guillotine in January 1793.

Space does not permit here a comprehensive assessment of the First French Republic and the most notorious phase of it, the Terror. This was the period of the Revolution which foreshadowed the totalitarian state of our own century. The ruling authority of the Terror was a board of twelve men called the Committee of Public Safety, whose dictatorial power, according to Gershoy, emanated from the Convention but whose leaders dominated the Convention for more than a year. The goal of the Terror was to mobilize all components of the state to the greatest possible degree for war, and to destroy counterrevolutionary elements from within and without. The Terror was preeminently a war government, and a revolutionary government as well in the sense that it was not founded on a constitution. To fulfill its goals, France during the Terror established the first *levée-en-masse*, mass levy of men, which forever changed the nature of warfare on the European continent. It imposed price controls, which amounted to a dramatic extension of state regulation into the economy. It attacked religion with an intensity not displayed by earlier revolutionary regimes. It condemned thousands of presumed enemies of the Revolution before tribunals which could only be termed "kangaroo courts." It dabbled, by means of terror and gaudy public spectacles, in thought control.

This was the period of the Revolution when liberty was freely sacrificed in the name of liberty. And it was memories of the Terror that made democracy a dirty word in Europe for generations because these bloody, chaotic months seemed to show that power in the hands of the people would simply mean *mobocracy*. Such was bound to be the case, as Edmund Burke had foretold in 1790, when the passions of individuals are unrestrained by an authority outside of themselves. "The effect of liberty to individuals," Burke wrote, "is that they may do what they please: We ought to see what it will please them to do," he continued, "before we risk congratulations, which may be soon turned into complaints." "The Terror *was* terrible," Robert Darnton writes in *The New York Review of Books*. "It was a trauma that scarred modern history at its birth." It has

17

also scarred attitudes toward the whole revolutionary experience in France.

This trauma passed in July 1794 when Robespierre and other principals in the Terror were toppled from power and guillotined in the first act of what has become known as the Thermidorean Reaction. A moderate government under the Directory followed, though this regime proved incapable of healing the deep divisions in French society and was besieged from both political extremes. One might have predicted, once 1792 arrived, that the final leader of the Revolutionary era would come from the military. In 1799, a young general named Bonaparte, fresh from victories in Italy and Egypt, seized power and harnessed the institutions of state more effectively than perhaps any French ruler before him. The debate about Napoleon, however, will forever be: "Did he destroy the Revolution or preserve it?" Did his authoritarian rule break faith with the ideals of 1789 or make it possible for those ideals to survive? Yet another riddle to ponder.

Finally, what are we to make of the complex drama of the Revolution? The French Revolution will always mean different things to different people, with the determining factor being, in all likelihood, one's own ideological predispositions. There is enough in the course of this event to attract or repulse just about anybody. Between 1789 and 1815, the revolutionary era, France produced six different constitutions embracing forms of government from limited monarchy to republicanism to military dictatorship. We cannot say that the Revolution bequeathed to France long-term political stability, for it has had thirteen different constitutions and at least five revolutions since 1789. Violence intruded on the process of political and social regeneration at numerous points. Much of the ideological and nationalistic warfare throughout Europe for a century to come could be traced directly to this period. Much of the promise of the French Revolution has remained unfulfilled. But the fact that Western societies today are even on the road toward ever greater degrees of liberty, equality, and fraternity must be explained in large part by the French Revolution. The idealism of the men of 1789 lit a beacon that still burns in the form of hope that political and social orders can improve themselves—that they can attain greater degrees of fairness and freedom—and in the form of an ongoing challenge that such improvements should be undertaken. That the French revolutionaries made wrong turns along this path should not besmirch what is noble about the vision they unleashed. May the Revolution remain a permanent thing, inspiring us by its ideals, and warning us by its excesses.

THE GODS OF REVOLUTION

JOHN WILLSON

John Willson has been a professor of history at Hillsdale College since 1975. He currently serves as a division chairman. A former presidentially-appointed member of the Board of Foreign Scholarships, a syndicated columnist, and a professor at St. Louis University, he has published articles in a number of journals, including Focus/Midwest, The Conservative Historian's Forum, Modern Age, Social Studies, *and* The University Bookman. *Recently* The Detroit Free Press *selected Dr. Willson as one of only four professors featured in an article on the best teachers in Michigan.*

THERE IS A story that comes under the heading, "if it isn't true, it should be." Otto von Hapsburg was walking on the Great Wall of China with Chou En-lai. The heir to an ancient European throne asked the Chinese premier, second in command in a much more ancient empire: "So, what do you think of the French Revolution?" Chou En-lai replied, "It's too soon to tell." *That's* perspective. We are accustomed in our culture to work with less.

One of the things we can say about the French in their revolutionary years is that they were good at arranging impressive ceremonies. Two scenes will suffice. First, the revolutionary events of 1789 actually began with a religious procession. The deputies of the Estates-General, scheduled to meet for the first time in 175 years, marched behind a processional cross to the Church of Saint Louis, at Versailles. The Third Estate, the commoners, came first, dressed in plain black; they were followed by the nobles in black and white satin, gold lace, and plumes; then the clergy. The Archbishop of Paris carried the Blessed Sacrament under a canopy; and finally came the King, wearing the coronation mantle. A mass of the Holy Spirit was sung at the church. It included, according to John McManners, author of *The French Revolution and the Church*, a sermon by the Bishop of Nancy, two hours long, as befitted the uniqueness and dignity of the occasion.

Four years and two months later Charlotte Corday stabbed Jean-Paul Marat to death, in his bath. This "venomous and diseased little Swiss doctor, who was regarded as either a criminal or a lunatic by the respectable politicians of the Assembly," reports Christopher Dawson in his book which provided the title of this essay, had become a revolutionary saint, although not of the type the Church would have recognized. His body was laid in republican state, and simple folk crowded by, also viewing his bloody shirt and the bath in which he expired. The Cordeliers (his radical political club) buried him in their garden in solemn ceremony. The next day the women of the revolutionary society took an oath to bring up their children in the cult of Marat and to give them no other scripture but his works. Finally, in the Cordelier's club-room, McManners writes, they celebrated the feast of the heart of Marat, where it was suspended in an urn from the roof, amidst applause.

The religion that sanctioned the events of 1789 was not the same religion that canonized Marat, but they were both religions nevertheless. By the time of Marat's murder (July 13, 1793) his religion had gone to war against the former King's religion, in the west of France, in the Vendee. France was also engaged in a holy war against her Christian neighbors, and soon would begin to apply "the nation's razor" to the necks of her internal enemies. Arnold Toynbee explains what had happened:

> In the Revolution a sinister ancient religion which
> had been dormant suddenly re-erupted with elemen-
> tal violence. This revenant was the fanatical worship
> of collective human power. The Terror was only the
> first of the mass-crimes that have been committed
> during the last hundred and seventy years in this evil
> religion's name.

The re-emergence of the "sinister ancient religion" called
forth vicious persecution of the religion that had shaped
the society the revolutionaries were trying to overthrow.

This is a problem of the modern age; it may even be *the*
problem of the modern age. It distances the French Revolution from the English and the American; it is central to
every revolution since the French. I intend to briefly discuss three revolutions besides the French, and try to show
how the religious question has affected them. This isn't a
religious history of modern revolutions: it is an attempt to
illustrate the importance of religion in *certain* modern
revolutions. In this respect, France is the prototype;
Russia is to France as the power of ten; Spain is the counterrevolution (which is why it was so irksome to Western
liberals); and Cuba is after-modern, a revolution that pre-
tends the new religion is already in place.

These revolutions have much in common. But these
remarks are not comparative: they are argumentative.
Crane Brinton's erudite and witty little book, *The Anatomy of Revolution*, is still a good comparative guide to
what's what in revolutions. I want to suggest that since the
soul of Western civilization has been the Judeo-Christian
religion, the great task of modern revolutionaries has been
to render it dead, or at least to consign it to the scrap heap
of history. I think here of the burial scene in the movie
Amadeus, when Mozart's genius is dropped uncere-
moniously into a lime-sprinkled mass grave. The irony for
our topic here is not only in Salieri's madness, the madness of mediocrity, but in the time. Mozart died shortly

22

after the Pope condemned the Civil Constitution of the Clergy in 1791, which touched off the religious war in France. The war continues to this day: traditional religion against the religion of man, the latter necessarily puny but enormously powerful in the material sense and in the short run. (Christopher Dawson in *The Gods of Revolution* and Erik Ritter von Kuehnelt-Leddihn in *Leftism: From Sade and Marx to Hitler and Pol Pot* have written extensively on this theme and my debt is to them.)

The French Revolution of 1789 was liberal and constitutional. It became bloodthirsty only gradually. The Revolution of 1789 brought monumental reforms, to be sure; but the spirit of Lafayette was in the air, and the bourgeoisie, the moderate nobility, and the reforming clergy thought they could control the course of events. Lafayette had watched his conservative American friends keep a lid on the boiling pot across the Atlantic. There was no reason, the French reformers thought, that they couldn't do the same. Their aim was "national unity," which they celebrated in the Feast of the Federation on July 14, 1790: Bastille Day. That such an ugly incident as the fall of an essentially unused prison and the murderous revelry it provoked should turn so quickly into a day of national celebration should have sounded warning bells to sober Frenchmen.

The Feast of the Federation was "a genuine act of national consecration to the new religion of patriotism and the ideals of Liberty, Equality, and Fraternity," says Dawson. Lafayette orchestrated it. The National Guard turned out from all 44,000 French municipalities; Bishop Talleyrand said mass at the Altar of the Fatherland, surrounded by 400 children, the King, and the National Assembly. Afterward they all swore the oath of federation. The young Wordsworth was visiting France for the first time at that very moment, and he immortalized the spirit of national unity in the *Prelude.*

Two days earlier (July 12, 1790), the Assembly had

passed the Civil Constitution of the Clergy. "If there was a point at which the Revolution 'went wrong,'" John McManners writes, "it was when the Constituent Assembly imposed the oath to the Civil Constitution of the Clergy, November 27, 1790. This marked the end of national unity, and the beginning of civil war." The law created the Constitutional Church. It bypassed the Pope in matters external to the faith, or the "civil" features of the Catholic religion. Bishops and priests became employees of the state, paid by the government and chosen by the people (it was even possible for non-believers and Protestants to vote). Dioceses were made congruent with political departments, parishes reduced in number and boundary lines made more "rational." It is important to note that under the *ancien régime* kings had claimed similar powers. The innovation in this aspect of the law was not primarily the encroachment of the secular power. It was rather the standardization of parish and diocesan life and democratization in the recruitment of clergy.

These changes affected only the "secular" clergy, or those in the parishes. The "regular" clergy, those in religious orders, *were abolished altogether*, with provisions made for pensions and an appropriate period of transition. Most nuns stayed in their orders; about half the monks welcomed their freedom. One major effect of this latter provision was to reduce the influence of the Church in education, welfare, and medical care (formerly the almost exclusive province of the regular clergy) to near zero. State eventually replaced Church in these crucial areas of French life.

Perhaps most important of all, the state imposed these changes without consulting the Church, and without consulting Rome. In a masterpiece of insensitivity, the historian R. R. Palmer says in *The World of the French Revolution,* "The adoption of all these measures naturally produced disagreements, both in the assembly and throughout the country." In fact, the law produced schism in the Church, led to the downfall of the King, and provoked the Reign of Terror.

The oath was administered at parish masses, beginning on January 2, 1791. Very few bishops took it, and most of the clergy were reluctant. The King had waffled for a month before sanctioning it, against his better judgment. The Pope considered it even longer, but finally published his condemnation of the entire law on May 4, declaring it "schismatic." It focused the matter. National unity began to come apart. Writing six decades later, Alexis de Tocqueville tried to put religion in the Revolution in perspective:

> One of the earliest enterprises of the revolutionary movement was a concerted attack on the Church, and among the many passions inflamed by it the first to be kindled and last to be extinguished was of an anti-religious nature.

An attack on the Church turned into anti-religious passion. Nevertheless, he says, we must distinguish between passions and *causes*. The Revolution was political. It *turned into* an anti-religious crusade because, "Tradition was fundamental to the whole conception of the Church," and the revolutionaries had nothing but contempt for tradition. Also, "The Church acknowledged an authority superior to human reason and was based on a hierarchy"; the revolutionaries made reason a god and "were for levelling out all differences between men." They were convinced that "in order to overthrow the institutions of the existing social order they must begin by destroying those of the Church." Whereas earlier political revolutions had usually respected the established faith, earlier religious revolutions had usually respected established political institutions.

Tocqueville notes:

> In the French Revolution, however, both religious institutions and the whole system of government were thrown into the melting pot, with the result that men's minds were in a state of utter confusion; they knew neither what to hold on to, nor when to stop. Revolutionaries of a hitherto unknown breed came on the scene: men who carried audacity to the point of sheer insanity; who balked at no innovation and, unchecked by any scruples, acted with an unprecedented ruthlessness.

Tocqueville is wrong when he argues that the revolutionaries had no religion to substitute for Christianity, but he sees the reasons for the anti-religious fury with his usual clarity.

Nor should the fury surprise us. The French Enlightenment had been fundamentally anti-Christian (and anti-Jewish, we might add) from the start. Insofar as the Revolution fed on Enlightenment ideas, it was implicitly anti-Christian even before the Civil Constitution of the Clergy opened new wounds. Peter Gay, certainly no friend to the Church, makes this very clear: he doesn't like the metaphor of a bridge from Christianity to the French *philosophes* because, says Gay in *The Enlightenment, An Interpretation:*

> The image of a bridge is helpful but incomplete; it fails to evoke the *essential* hostility between eighteenth-century religion and eighteenth-century secularism: the *philosophes* rudely treated the Christian past rather as Voltaire treated the plays of Shakespeare—as a dunghill strewn with diamonds, crying out to be pillaged and badly needing to be cleaned out.

The *philosophes* had two enemies, Gay continues: "the institutions of Christianity and the idea of hierarchy." And they were also trying "to undermine the Christian view of man and of morality." In *The Party of Humanity*, Gay argues that they intended to "expose *l'infame* [this refers to Voltaire's slogan, *ecrasez l'infame*] loudly, repeatedly, insistently, unsparingly" until the tepid Christian public was persuaded. And in *The Enlightenment*, Gay notes that they were determined to ridicule Christianity "with all possible brutality." There was not a gentle bone in the body of the *philosophes'* writing, and there would not be a gentle bone in the bodies of their children, the revolutionaries.

Furthermore, Ernst Cassirer has emphasized that the "essential, unifying conviction of the Enlightenment . . . was the rejection of the idea of original sin." A twist on this, adds Gay, is Rousseau's "one great principle"—"that man is good, that society makes him bad, but that only society, the agent of perdition, can be the agent of salvation." Rousseau is a special case, and should not normally be thrown together with the *philosophes*, but here the point is this: with a man-centered set of convictions surrounding the revolutionaries, it took only refractory priests to call forth the revolutionaries' fury and to clarify the new religion of man.

One problem was that the Constitutional church was no more acceptable to real radicals than the Roman Catholic Church had been. So when refractory priests and peasants clung to the old, the reformers all the more savagely cleared the way for the new. Thirty to forty thousand non-juring (those refusing to take the oath) priests emigrated. At least two, and perhaps as many as five thousand priests were executed under the Terror. In Lyon, in November 1793, 135 priests and monks were massacred; 83 were shot in one day near Angers; there were mass drownings at Nantes; and at Rochefort, of the 850 priests imprisoned on three old slaver-ships, 274 survived. Nuns died too: 16 Carmelites of Compiegne, sisters of Charity in Arras, Ursulines at Valenciennes; what danger could they have been to the republic? Seven nuns were dispatched by guillotine from May to July 1794: three had refused to name the refractory priest who had been saying mass for them, one had corresponded with her brother in exile, another had a "royalist" pamphlet in her possession, and the abbess of Montmarte, 72 years of age, they said had made "exactions" on her "vassals." The Abbé Pinot mounted the scaffold in his ecclesiastical vestments; on his lips were the words "Introibo ad altare Dei," ("I will go to the altar of God.")

This scene, recounted by McManners, reminds us that in our "zeal for statistics . . . we must beware of making trivial the overwhelming business of dying." And Frenchmen died in horrible numbers: perhaps a quarter million in the Vendée, in a civil war within a civil war that did not stop until Napoleon's pact with the Pope a decade later. "It was by making myself a Catholic that I finished the war in the Vendée," he said. Thus he recognized what every Frenchman knew at the time: it was a *religious* war. Its ferocity can be explained in no other way. As one Jacobin officer put it, "What is the good of tactics against men who fight with a rosary and a scapular in their hands and throw themselves on our artillery armed with nothing but sticks?" The wretches were insensible to any kind of reason, he concluded, so the only proper course was "to kill them all, or they will kill us."

A man who embodies many of the sordid features of the Terror is the "butcher of Arras," Joseph Lebon. He was an Oratorian who welcomed his chance for freedom under the Civil Constitution of the Clergy, and who seized the ideas of Rousseau even more fervently than he had once embraced his religious vows. Although he hated priests, he became a *curé* in the Constitutional Church, for a while even exhibiting real tolerance for his refractory predecessor. He married when that became an option, and later tried to force other priests to marry as a sign of their support for the new order (one of the many little tragedies of the era was the vulnerability even of juring clergy to the ever-changing whims of the revolutionary leadership). "If, when the revolution is over," he came to feel, "we still have the poor with us, our revolutionary toils will have been in vain."

When he gained control of the Terror in Arras, he put his passionate allegiance to the Revolution into particularly sadistic action. A slogan said, "As long as there is one priest left on the soil of the Republic, liberty will not have won a total victory." Lebon boasted that there was not a single one left in his province. He set up his guillotine in front of the theater, from whose balcony he and his wife could watch the executions. It is said that he read the local newspaper to one marquis (whose misfortune was to have been among the "rich") who was in position and waiting for the knife to fall, and then exhorted him to carry news of revolutionary military victories into the next world.

The Revolution devoured many of its most ardent functionaries. At his trial during the Thermidorian Reaction to the Terror, Lebon said, "I derived most of my revolutionary maxims from the Gospels which, from beginning to end, preach against the rich and against priests." But he was not simply an anti-clerical lover of the poor. He was determined to usher in the age of virtue and the religion of man. To do that, he had to wipe out priests, but he also had to eradicate the Church. Lebon is an example of a phenomenon that became common in twentieth-century revolutions. Kuehnelt-Leddihn puts it this way: "The perversion of basic Christian sentiments comes easily to silly priests who have neglected their spiritual life, and secularizing theology, become real mobmasters, as it now so frequently happens in Latin America."

An important part of the Terror was de-Christianization, which was meant to preceed the true enlightened age.

Interestingly, the most ardent champion of the religion of
virtue, Maximilien Robespierre, advocated caution when
it came to desecrating churches, murdering priests, and
other extreme action. He operated on the principle of Talleyrand, who, when he heard about Napoleon's order to
have a duke assassinated, cried, "It is worse than a crime!
It is a mistake!" The Terror perpetrated many "mistakes,"
Robespierre to the contrary notwithstanding.

De-Christianization was bewildering in its variety.
There was a form for almost every locality, and historians
have tended to dilute its viciousness by studying its com-
plexity. But it comes down to three principles which have
lived into the revolutions of our own day.

1) *Violence against clergy and churches.* Whether sponsored by *curés rouges*, anti-clerical mobs, revolutionary
armies, local politicians, or Jacobin societies, violence
happened everywhere, at least in the early stages of the
Terror. Revolutionaries made war on vestments and holy
relics, especially; they closed churches or converted them
to military or bureaucratic uses; they desecrated religious
objects (mutilated statues, ripped down crosses; the small
acts being even more telling, such as the committee in
Aix-en-Provence boasting to the Convention about "the
cross of silvered wood we are using at the moment as a
broom handle"); they occasionally danced naked in the
ruined churches or drank from the communion vessels;
and they also murdered people. McManners says:

> Like the execution of the King, sacrilege was to be a
> gesture of defiance, a symbol of the determination to
> destroy the old world, a deliberate decision to press
> on beyond the point of no return, a final commitment
> to the oath to "live free or die."

2) *Legislative and bureaucratic policies designed to
make it difficult for religious institutions to function.*
Non-juring clergy were assumed to be counterrevolution-

aries; even Constitutional clergy could be banished if any six citizens brought charges against them for any reason. Priests often were forced to marry. The army requisitioned church bells, railings, and ornaments for the war effort, and religious buildings for offices and headquarters. This was something new under the sun: religion was subject to politics, because *everything* was subject to politics.

3) *New civic religion imposed by the state.* "It was not enough to bind the carcase of the old church to the new state," says Christopher Dawson. "What the Revolution demanded was a new civic religion which would be entirely *totalitarian in spirit* and which would recognize no higher duty than the service of the state." [Emphasis mine.] Louis XVI had remarked when a particularly notorious Constitutional priest was put up for Archbishop of Paris that it would be better if a man in that position believed in God. Once Robespierre began setting the religious agenda, belief in any god but reason and the state became automatic disqualification for any public position. French revolutionaries did not develop a religious ideology as fully blown as, say, Lenin's, but what they had was a religion nonetheless, as Dawson points out:

> Like Christianity, it was a religion of human salvation, the salvation of the world by the power of man set free by Reason. The Cross has been replaced by the tree of Liberty, the Grace of God by the Reason of Man, and Redemption by Revolution.

They changed the calendar, so as to eliminate the Sabbath and to institute the more reasonable *decadi* based on cycles of ten. They made the churches into "Temples of Reason." Poupinel, a writer of republican hymns, said, "let us use civic pomp to make people forget the old displays of superstition . . . and the skeleton of sacerdotalism will disintegrate of its own accord." On November 10, 1793, Robespierre sponsored a Festival of Reason in the cathedral of Notre Dame. Inside was a "Mountain," with a temple of "Philosophy" at the summit, from which emerged a goddess of "Liberty." It was shabby and naïve. Later revolutionaries would get much better at it.

Priests in particular, and Christians in general, had it even tougher in Russia. The Russian revolutionaries didn't add much to what the Jacobins had invented, but they did take everything up to at least the power of ten. In *Three Who Made a Revolution*, Bertram Wolfe assigns to them "a fanaticism that served as a surrogate for the older religions":

> It idealized Russia, the peasant, the proletariat, science, the machine. It made a true gospel of its particular brand of salvation. It possessed singleness, exclusivism, dogma, orthodoxy, heresy, regeneration, schism, excommunication, prophets, disciples, vocation, asceticism, sacrifice, the ability to suffer all things for the sake of the faith. Heresy or rival doctrine was worse than ignorance; it was apostasy.

Crane Brinton feels that although the Bolsheviks hated the Orthodox Church as hard as Jacobins hated Catholics, "one gets the impression that in Russia sheer terrorism directed against organized Christianity was not quite as intense as it had been in France." That would surprise the priests. Lenin and Stalin had 42,000 of them killed between the Bolshevik Revolution of 1917 and the outbreak of World War II in 1939. There were 60,000 priests as late as 1930. By 1941, only 3,000 remained. Under Khrushchev, only about a hundred churches remained open. The historian Robert Conquest has shown how difficult it is to get numbers out of Russia, but *at the very least*, the Russians killed as many priests in relation to the total population as the French. And they desecrated churches every bit as enthusiastically.

But that isn't really the point. During the ill-fated revolution of 1905, Lenin decided that being anticlerical wasn't enough: Bolsheviks had to destroy *all past religions.* "Communism, like Jacobinism before it," says Brinton, "takes very seriously its anti-Christian mission." Although Lenin had his hands full with other things during the period of civil war, by 1922 he ordered the secret police to carry out a "church revolution." They worked with two organizations for many years. The "Living Church" movement was to Russia what the Constitutional Church had been in France; it was collaborationist, but not *necessarily* dishonorable. The "League of the Militant Godless," on the other hand, was something like the Red Guards of the Chinese Cultural Revolution. Its members were young, ideological, devoted to the revolution, willing to hound the church into obscurity. The full machinery of what Solzhenitsyn calls "our sewage disposal system" was put into operation, aiming for the "root destruction of religion in the country."

The Soviet constitution guaranteed freedom of worship, but as the poet Tanya Khodkevich wrote:

> You can pray *freely*
> But just so God alone can hear.

She received a ten-year sentence for these verses. They arrested the Patriarch, metropolitans and bishops, priests and deacons, and *rarely reported the arrests to the press.* "The circles kept getting bigger," says Solzhenitsyn, "as they raked in ordinary believers as well, old people, and particularly women, who were the most stubborn believers of all." Religious education of children was classified as counterrevolutionary propaganda. Religious prisoners could not return to their children or their home areas after their release. Christians were shot for "agitating" to reopen previously closed churches, for publishing prayers in Old Slavonic, for conspiring to protect the Patriarch (the theory was, that since the Patriarch was in no danger, conspiring to protect him was implicitly critical of the government and therefore counterrevolutionary), and witholding relics from the state program of confiscation. Solzhenitsyn cries out:

> There was a multitude of Christians: prisoner transports and graveyards, prisoner transports and graveyards. Who will count those millions? They died unknown, casting only in their immediate vicinity a light like a candle. They were the best of Russia's Christians. The worst had all . . . trembled, recanted, and gone into hiding.

The persecution kept up, year after year, shifting slightly, lessening a little, emphasizing now the Orthodox, later the Catholics, still later the Baptists. If one gets the impression that it was less intense in Russia than in France, perhaps it is the contrast between the red passion of the ex-priest Lebon, with his bloody guillotine, and the crude stubborness of the ex-seminarian, Stalin, smashing believers into the Russian snow with a muddy boot.

If you have a taste for passionate intensity, it is to Spain's revolution that you should turn. We have been taught to think of the Spanish Civil War as peculiarly modern, the struggle between democracy and fascism, a rehearsal for the Second World War. In fact, as *The Spanish Civil War as a Religious Tragedy* by Jose M. Sanchez puts it, "The Spanish War was the greatest and last struggle between traditional triumphalist Catholicism and liberal-proletarian secularism." The only quibble I have is with the word "proletarian." It had nothing to do with workers. Spain's revolution started and stopped several times, then got under way again in 1931. At that point it was liberal and constitutional. But unlike France in 1789, Spain was *very* Catholic. The great Spanish philosopher Miguel de Unamuno said, "Here in Spain we are all Catholics, even the atheists." A center-right government elected in 1935 turned into a Popular Front in 1936, which produced several reactions, the most important being the army's revolt (a very Spanish tradition) of 1936, followed by a leftist fury against religion and the Church's full support of what quickly became a counterrevolution.

Sanchez says that by late 1936 "the religious issue had caused complete polarization. Anticlerical violence had created violent clericals." The anticlerical fury of 1936 was "an anticlerical attack unsurpassed in all history." Anticlericalism was a permanent feature of the very clerical Spain, and had been a part of every liberal or leftist uprising since 1800. But in this case the defenders of liberal democracy, as the Trotskyist Andres Nin put it, "solved the problem of the Church very simply; [they left not] a one standing." Almost 7,000 clerics were murdered; in relative terms more than in France, or even Russia. Probably the Romans did not eliminate as high a percentage of the early Christian leaders. Everything happened that one can imagine: desecration of churches, rapes and murders of nuns, graves violated, religious objects mutilated, hideous torture, and countless murders of lay Christians for their faith. Almost incredibly, Sanchez writes, on occasion "priests would be given an opportunity to save themselves by apostasizing, by denying their faith, but *there is no record of any of them having done so.*"

This all happened in the government zones, the areas controlled by what most Western foreigners thought was the "legitimate" government. Meanwhile, the opposition which came to call itself "Nationalist" got the support of the Church, because "the conflict was indeed a religious war." *Despite* help from Hitler's Germany and Mussolini's Italy (and pressures from internal fascists), the Nationalist movement of General Francisco Franco managed to keep its independence. The Church, while not necessarily approving of the Nationalist army's allies or its brutality, recognized that the war was not one of progress versus superstition. Instead, it spoke in favor of order against anarchy; in the words of Archbishop Pla y Deniel, "in favor of the defense of Christian civilization and its bases, religion, fatherland, and family, against those without God and against God." A Collective Letter went out from the Spanish bishops in 1937. It made the spiritual and cultural legacy of Spain the most important pillar of the Nationalist movement, whatever one thought of Franco or his allies. Like something out of the Vendée, Spanish priests actually fought their enemies. One captive said that killing had nothing to do with his actions. "Today, it is not a matter of fulfilling God's commandments, rather, it is a question of wanting God to live in the souls of the people."

All the good-hearted liberals and communists from England and the United States who fought against the Nationalists in the Abraham Lincoln and International Brigades thought they were on the side of democracy and progress. Perhaps they were. But the English archbishop of Westminster was closer to the truth when he insisted that "all who are not willfully blind see the battle raging between Christian civilization and the worst form of paganism that has ever darkened the earth." Spain has given the world the only (temporarily) successful counterrevolution since 1789.

Christians re-converted to revolutionary faith have popped up in every modern upheaval. Joseph Lebon was a creation of the French Revolution, but he was by no means unique to it. But his type wants to *crush* the Church: Fidel Castro wants to *absorb* it. His manifesto, *History Will Absolve Me*, contains a classical statement of the merger of Christian and revolutionary eschatologies (here summarized by James Billington):

> He represented his own original revolutionary assault on the Moncado barracks as a kind of Incarnation. The subsequent torture and martyrdom of his virile fellow revolutionaries was the Passion and

Crucifixion; and Castro's trial by Batista was Christ before Pilate. The Cuban people were promised corporate Resurrection, and their revolutionary apostles Pentecostal power; the coming revolution would fulfill all the Law (the five "revolutionary laws" of the Moncado raiders) and the Prophets (Jose Marti).

When a pastoral letter signed by all the Cuban bishops denounced his regime, and a Catholic crowd chanted *"Cuba si, Communismo no!"* Castro responded that "whoever condemns a revolution such as ours betrays Christ and would be capable of crucifying Him again."

Because the Church did oppose *his* Coming, Castro at first persecuted it. The revolution confiscated all Catholic hospitals, asylums, social centers, and schools. It closed down the Catholic university of St. Thomas of Villanova. It abolished saints' days, holy week, Epiphany, and even Christmas. About 3,000 priests left the country, and many others were forced out of their vocation. The Archbishop of Havana had to seek asylum in the Argentine Embassy, and he died without ever returning to his office. The police made lists of those who went to church.

But once he tamed the Church by force, Castro began to woo it, linking the New Man of Cuban socialism with the New Man of Christian theology. The new world is here, he began to say; the Church is a part of it! Instead of eradicating the Church, the revolution *appropriated it.* First Castro had faked religion; later he opposed it and persecuted it; then he ignored it. But this was his triumph, and what he added to the world the French revolutionaries created: he *fused* Marxism and Christianity, and thus found the way to make the Church irrelevant, the mere lapdog of the revolution. Joseph Lebon would be green with envy.

So, to a twentieth century revolutionary like Chou En-lai, it may well be "too soon to tell" about the French Revolution. There is still a disturbing amount of traditional religion around, and in some places it is pretty strong. But Christopher Dawson knew that "a free society requires a higher degree of spiritual unity than a totalitarian one. Hence the spiritual integration of Western culture is essential to its temporal survival." Probably all the real revolutionaries since 1789 have understood that too; for both sides the outcome is as yet uncertain. We would do well to keep in mind the words of Joseph de Maistre, a deeply traditional Christian ("contempt of Locke is the beginning of wisdom," he paraphrased Proverbs), as he observed the world aflame with Terror in 1794: "What we are witnessing, is a religious revolution; the rest, immense as it seems, is but an appendix."

Chronology of Religion in the French Revolution

1789

May 4	Procession and mass for opening of Estates-General
July 14	Fall of Bastille
August 4	Orders renounce feudal privileges
August 11	Clergy abandon tithes
November 2	Church property "at the disposal of the nation"

1790

April 12	Dom Gerle's motion for Catholicism as "religion of the state" defeated
July 12	Civil Constitution of the Clergy voted
July 14	First Feast of the Federation
November 27	Decree imposing clerical oath
December 26	King reluctantly sanctions decree

1791

| January 2 | Oath-taking begins at parish masses |

Chronology of Religion in the French Revolution (*cont'd.*)

March 21	Papal Nuncio hands over Pope's condemnation of Civil Constitution of the Clergy
May 4	Pope publishes condemnation
June 20	King's flight to Varennes
July 11	Voltaire's bones interred in Pantheon
July 14	Second Feast of the Federation
July 17	Massacre of Champ de Mars
November 29	Decree making non-jurors "suspects"
December 19	King vetoes decree against non-jurors

1792

April 15	Festival of Liberty
May 26	New decree against refractory priests (vetoed)
August 10	Fall of the King
August 14	Further decrees against clergy
September 2	Prison massacres
December 20	Trial of King

1793

January 21	Execution of King
March 10	Revolt in the Vendée
April 6	Creation of Committee of Public Safety
August 10	Festival of new constitution
October 1	De-Christianization at Abbeville
October 7	Revolutionary calendar adopted
October 16	Execution of Queen
November 10	Festival of Reason in cathedral of Notre-Dame

1794

May 7	Cult of the Supreme Being
June 8	Festival of the Supreme Being

Chronology of Religion in the French Revolution (*cont'd.*)

July 28   Execution of Robespierre
November 12 Jacobin Club closed

1795

February 21   Decree of Boissy d'Anglas (separation of
              church and state)
September   New oath on clergy
October 26   Directory

EDMUND BURKE, JEAN-JACQUES ROUSSEAU, AND THE FRENCH REVOLUTION

PETER J. STANLIS

Peter J. Stanlis has taught in colleges and universities around the world for more than forty years. He has published over a hundred articles and nine books, his best known being Edmund Burke and the Natural Law (*University of Michigan Press, 1958*), *which has been credited with revolutionizing modern scholarship on Burke. He is also the co-author of* Edmund Burke: A Bibliography of Secondary Studies to 1982 (*Garland Publishing, 1983*) *and editor of* Edmund Burke: Selected Writings and Speeches (*Regnery Gateway, 1963*). *A member of the National Council for the Humanities from 1982 to 1988 and a British Academy Fellow, Dr. Stanlis is Distinguished Professor Emeritus of Humanities at Rockford College.*

$\mathbb{M}$Y SUBJECT IS Burke, Rousseau, and the French Revolution, and one could devote hundreds of pages to each aspect of this subject. Therefore, I shall limit myself pretty much to the views toward history held by Burke and Rousseau, and also to their respective views of human nature in relationship to the nature and function of civil and social institutions. This narrows down the subject to something manageable.

It is unfortunate that most readers of Burke's *Reflections*, including those who agree with his basic political philosophy, perceive this work as primarily an attack on the French Revolution, and not as a defense of European and Western civilization. It is much easier, I am sure, to perceive what Burke was attacking than what he was defending. Significantly, those readers who have most seriously misunderstood the *Reflections* are the very ones who have paid the least attention to what he was defending. Because of their limited understanding of Burke's politics, the positive principles in his political and social philosophy, which provide the foundation of his attack on the French Revolution, simply elude them.

The most common fallacy in this regard is that Burke was defending the established status quo in France against any reforms; that he was the champion of the supposedly absolute monarchy, with all its abuses and powers, real or imagined; that he was defending the nobility, with its special feudal privileges such as exemption from certain taxes and other social obligations; that in objecting to the confiscation of Church property and the persecution of the clergy he was defending privileges which were held to violate the rights of conscience and freedom of religion of those outside the Church. This common approach to Burke by ardent defenders of the Revolution, including academic Marxist and liberal historians in the tradition of positivist scholarship, dismisses him as a kind of superstitious obfuscationist whose specious arguments stand in the way of "progress" toward liberty, equality, and fraternity, which the Revolution claimed to establish. In short, Burke is pictured as an enemy of democracy.

Consistent with this view, such critics dismiss Burke's claim that the essence of the French Revolution is to be found in its atheism, and in its rationalistic, speculative, abstract ideology derived from the writers of the Enlightenment. Burke's interpretation of the Revolution is categorically denied or largely ignored by many of these critics, particularly the Marxists.

The most immediate object of Burke's positive defense, in the *Reflections*, is saving Britain from adopting the principles of the French Revolution, by distinguishing the English Revolution of 1688 from the French Revolution. Burke made a strong case that the two revolutions were absolutely different. In fact, he defines the Revolution of 1688 as a revolution not made but prevented. He holds that the real would-be revolutionist was King James II, who aimed at violating the English constitution in church and state. The English aristocracy, lawyers, and military officers who forced the king to abdicate were defending the English constitution; they did so from necessity, and did not change the basic structure of the British state, but preserved it. In contrast, the French revolutionists aimed at destroying the inherited structure of the French state, and all the basic institutions of society which supported it.

Burke's positive defense of European and Western civilization can be traced back to one of his earliest writings, his satirical tract *A Vindication of Natural Society* (1756). In attacking those political theorists who thought it was possible and desirable to establish a "natural society," such as was thought to exist before European civil society became organized, in a fictitious pre-civil "state of nature," Burke was implicitly defending the real historically developed civilization of Europe. In the same year that he satirized the fictions of "natural society," he wrote *An Essay towards an Abridgement of the English History*, in which he set forth his serious views on the origins and development of European society, his views on man's historical past, and his conception of the moral nature of man.

Although Burke's *Abridgement of English History* was not published until 1812, fifteen years after his death, the importance of this early work for insights into his intellectual development and his political and social philosophy can hardly be overestimated. His English history reveals an extensive knowledge of both English and European society, from the ancient Roman period to the late Middle Ages. More importantly, the work supplies the first explicit evidence of his profound respect for the historical method of Montesquieu as applied to civil society. Burke's method in approaching social problems was both normatively ethical, through the moral natural law, and historically empirical, a method wholly at variance with Cartesian rationalism, based upon original total doubt, which largely ignored history. Despite all of their differences with Descartes, the abstract, speculative theorizing of such writers as Hobbes, Locke, and Rousseau have this in common: they all ignore or denigrate history, the approach to society which was to permeate almost every page that Burke wrote on politics and social problems. To Burke, the only reliable evidence on man as a civil-social animal was within the historical record, in man's experience, not in any imaginary or hypothetical pre-civil "state of nature" or social contract before society existed.

To advocate a return to a supposedly idyllic "state of nature" for the ethical norms by which men lived in an historically developed civil society was to Burke a highly dangerous illusion. Neither in such a supposedly idyllic "state of nature" (which Burke believed was a jungle and not a Garden of Eden), nor in organized civil society is there such a condition for mankind as Rousseau's "natural equality." Burke knew that natural equality can come into existence and be maintained only through revolutionary force, by levelling out all innate and acquired differences. In 1756 Burke knew that the pursuit of a fictitious natural equality, such as the French Revolutionists launched in 1789–90, would lead to violence and the destruction of social order.

In his *Abridgement of English History,* Burke clearly identified the chief elements that in various combinations and in different provinces and nations of Europe comprised the foundations of European civilization. They were the ancient Greco-Roman culture, particularly Roman civil law as embodied in the Justinian code, which gave a common law to Europe; the Christian religion, which included the Judaic morality of the Old Testament's Ten Commandments; and the customs and manners of the Germanic peoples who overran the Roman Empire. These three elements provided the legal, moral, religious, and social norms for European civilization, in the development of society from the fall of the Roman Empire to Burke's time, and they always commanded his veneration and respect. They were embodied in family, church, and state, and they infused provincial and national loyalties in every minor corporate institution of society, providing what Burke called the "moral clothing" of mankind.

Burke believed that the institutions of civil society were absolutely essential as the instrumental means of bringing human nature to some degree of its potential perfection. The basic institutions of society were the necessary means of providing the moral, intellectual, aesthetic, and social development of individuals and nations, through a normative value system common to Western civilization. Burke's view of the origins and historical development of European society is practically identical with that of Christopher Dawson, whose book *The Making of Europe* (1932), is largely a refinement of the principles in Burke's *Abridgement of English History.*

Because of his veneration of tradition and history, Burke has sometimes been called an historicist. The late Professor Leo Strauss and many of his students have argued that Burke is a kind of moral relativist, because his appeals to history make him accept without serious question whatever happens in history, including political despotism. This argument is simply false, and shows a serious misunderstanding of Burke's political philosophy, as well as of his political career. Strauss and his students have totally ignored the vital place of the moral natural law in Burke's politics.

Of all political thinkers or statesmen, Burke is among the very last who would be guilty of a moral relativism based upon historicism. His conception of history goes far beyond empirical facts, and is ultimately providential. It has seldom been noted that his early appeal to the three basic elements in European civilization reappears in his writings on the French Revolution. During the 1790s he noted the similitude throughout Europe of religion, laws, and manners, the very three elements that he identified as basic to Europe thirty-five years earlier, which he said comprised the aggregate of nations in the European commonwealth. He again noted that the nations of the Christian world have grown up to their present magnitude in a great length of time and by a great variety of developments.

In his writings on the French Revolution Burke noted that this Classical-Christian-Germanic system of civil society permeated the corporate nature of man as a civil-social creature, and was transmitted through tradition and history to each new generation of Europeans. Together with the moral natural law it provided the norms by which Burke judged important changes in society, such as the French Revolution. The "right reason" of the natural law, together with the circumstances of history, provided the basis for Burke's principle of prudence, which he frequently said is the first of moral and political virtues in the practical affairs of men in society. Whatever else can be said about the French Revolution, both its admirers and its critics should agree that it violated completely the spirit and letter of Burke's cardinal principle of prudence.

Burke's calling prudence the first of moral and political virtues is not to be taken lightly. To accept the established system of European society, which involves a reverence for the wisdom and achievements of our ancestors, does not preclude social and political reform of abuses. All true reform begins with an acceptance of present conditions; the situation of man is the preceptor of his duties. Reform is the opposite of revolution, and involves respect for the diverse classes and interests of society, with the aim of harmonizing their differences while retaining their civil rights. Burke argued that sudden revolutionary attempts to level out all individual and corporate distinctions, in the name of natural equality or any other revolutionary appeal, violates prudence and results in disorder and injustice. Prudence, on the other hand, safeguards the constitutional order in each nation and makes genuine reform possible without violent revolution.

Burke referred to the historical process by which the constitutions of European nations developed in each society as "working after the pattern of nature." Through the deliberate election of ages and generations, the slow organic growth of European institutions and nations had evolved to their present degree of improvement. The end result of what happens to human nature when it submits to the process of normative nature transmitted through tradition and history is described by Burke as follows:

> Every sort of moral, every sort of rational and natural ties that connect the human understanding and affections to the divine are no more than necessary to build up that wonderful structure: man; whose prerogative it is to be in a great degree a creature of his own making, and who, when made as he ought to be made, is destined to hold no trivial place in the creation.

This passage from the *Reflections* and others like it certainly indicates that Burke believed that the gradual unfolding of the Christian commonwealth of European nations, as he called it, was a process by which the human condition could be improved.

Burke had no philosophy of history, but his views on the past reveal a conception of man's place in temporal events, under the mysterious dispensations of God, that connects his view of history with his religion and his political philosophy. The common unity throughout the Christian commonwealth of Europe of laws, morals, manners, and customs, though modified by the particular circumstances of each nation, was for him the product of a slow historical development. It was an evolutionary process by which those who wielded power in church and state and other institutions acted in trust, and were accountable to both God and mankind. Abuses of power, or the refusal to eliminate abuses once established, was the result of the corruption or weaknesses of human nature itself, and not to be charged to the basic institutions of society.

Burke was convinced that no society or system of government could ever be totally free from corruption, much less arrive at any high degree of abstract perfection. These were utopian illusions such as were held by Rousseauists and believers in the natural goodness of man. As a Christian, Burke was aware of the imperfections and weaknesses of human nature, and knew that men in general, and particularly men in power, were tempted to fall into one or another or several of the seven deadly sins. On one occasion Burke said: "It is certainly no soothing news to me that large bodies of men are incurably corrupt." Yet at the same time he held out great hope that the kinds of corruption which filled the pages of history could be overcome by individuals with great moral integrity, and that the conditions of men in society could be improved through science and adherence to natural law and constitutional legal restraints on power. He did not believe that history contained any law of necessary "progress," but he did believe that improvements in the uses of power could occur, and that European society over the centuries down to his own time had improved in many ways.

In June 1988, I attended a conference on Rousseau at Columbia University, and made some of these points and referred to the Christian Commonwealth of Europe that Burke described. I received howls of derision from the conferees, who were all enthusiastic Rousseauists and had no use at all for Burke. A kind of mindless euphoria seemed to seize them whenever Rousseau's political ideas were set forth, and I found it almost impossible to conduct any kind of rational discourse with them. The same kind of response occurred two years later, at another conference on Rousseau, when I questioned Rousseau's contention that ignorance, not knowledge, is the basis of virtue.

A similar kind of phenomenon has characterized the conspiracy of silence by many Marxist and liberal academic historians who refuse to deal with the counter-revolution in France, to ignore it completely, as though it never happened, or at best to refer to it in passing, in order to condemn it. It is not always easy to determine whether their silence is from moral corruption in principle, or cowardliness, or intellectual dishonesty, but the total effect is to write history as ideological propaganda. Needless to say, the Marxist critics of our time have generally ignored Burke. But several who have dealt with him, such as C. B. Macpherson and Christopher Reid, have screened him through the Marxist ideology of class warfare, with results that warp any possible understanding of Burke on his own terms. To understand Burke's writings on the French Revolution it is necessary to know his entire political and social philosophy, including his views of history and his convictions concerning the origins, nature, and function of the basic institutions of society, and his conception of the moral nature of man.

49

As an Aristotelian, who believed that man is by his nature a social and political animal, Burke regarded the so-called "artificial" institutions of society as "natural" in the sense of normal. He put this in the form of an aphorism: "Art is man's nature." When Burke discussed institutions he identified them with the corporate nature of man. He rejected as invalid the revolutionary conception of man in terms of numbers. Men did not identify themselves in terms of majorities and minorities, but rather in terms of their identity in family, church, nationality, profession, race, sex, age, and through their allegiance to various corporate bodies. He also looked upon human nature in terms of its acquired characteristics, developed from their innate potential for good or evil, for their power to create or appreciate the beautiful and the true, as opposed to the ugly and the false. Acquired characteristics were the result of education and the process of living in society as members of one or more institutions, and the potential of man, positively or negatively, appeared very considerable to Burke. Whether or not an individual developed to his full potential depended upon how he made use of all the aids to grace that were available to him in organized civil society.

In the second edition of his satire, *A Vindication of Natural Society* (1757), Burke implicitly raised the question: what would happen if humanity were stripped of all its institutions, of all the props to government, which proponents of "natural society" argued were unnecessary, or impediments to liberty, through their paradoxical and imaginary, but plausible, arguments. The following passage is not only Burke's rebuttal of "natural society," but contains much that is found in his attacks on the French Revolution thirty-three years later:

> It is far more easy to maintain a wrong cause, and to support paradoxical opinions to the satisfaction of a

common auditory, than to establish a doubtful truth by solid and conclusive arguments. When men find that something can be said in favor of what, on the very proposal, they have thought utterly indefensible, they grow doubtful of their own reason; they are thrown into a sort of pleasing surprise; they run along with the speaker, charmed and captivated to find such a plentiful harvest of reasoning, where all seemed barren and unpromising. This is the fairy land of philosophy. And it very frequently happens, that those pleasing impressions on the imagination subsist and produce their effect, even after the understanding has been satisfied of their unsubstantial nature. There is a sort of gloss upon ingenious falsehoods that dazzles the imagination, but which neither belongs to, nor becomes the sober aspect of truth. . . . A mind which has no restraint from a sense of its own weakness, of its subordinate rank in the creation, and of the extreme danger of letting the imagination loose upon some subjects, may very plausibly attack everything the most excellent and venerable; that it would not be difficult to criticise the creation itself; and that if we were to examine the divine fabrics by our ideas of reason and fitness, and to use the same method of attack by which some men have assaulted revealed religion, we might with as good color, and with the same success, make the wisdom and power of God in his creation appear to many no better than foolishness. There is an air of plausibility which accompanies vulgar reasonings and notions, taken from the beaten circle of ordinary experience, that is admirably suited to the narrow capacities of some, and to the laziness of others. . . . Even in matters which are, as it were, just within our reach, what would become of the world, if the practice of all moral duties, and the foundations of society, rested upon having their reasons made clear and demonstrative to every individual?

In any consideration of the innate and acquired moral nature of man, Burke's question is extremely crucial, and it applies with special force to ideological revolutions based upon speculative reason. Burke's savage criticism of the French Revolution is his own answer to that rhetorical question. To put the same point as a declarative statement, Burke believed that if revolutionists strip society of all the institutional props, manners, customs, and laws inherited from the past, and leave men with nothing but their private reason, passions, and interests, they are inviting chaos, anarchy, confusion, violence, and all of the other characteristics that came to prevail in the French Revolution.

Contrary to what some academic historians have claimed, Burke was thoroughly knowledgeable of what transpired in the cultural and political life of France prior to and during the Revolution. He did not hold to a simplistic conspiratorial theory of the origins of the Revolution. Although he specifically identified the rationalism of the *philosophes* and the sensibility of Rousseau as specific causes, he knew that the complex of origins was far more inclusive than the ideas of philosophy and literature. This is an aspect of Burke's thought that needs to be explored much further. The full scope of his knowledge of France prior to and during the Revolution may be secured only by a thorough study of the *Annual Register* from its beginning in 1759 until 1796; by examining his private correspondence up to his death in 1797; and by his published writings and speeches on the Revolution. It would take a substantial book to do this, but such a study would illuminate much more thoroughly than has ever been done the extent to which Burke was aware of all the essential elements that caused the French Revolution, and shaped its direction and destiny. It would also determine far more conclusively whether the current academic historians who discount the philosophy of the Enlightenment as an important cause of the Revolution are justified in their claim.

Although Burke stressed that the philosophy of the Enlightenment was a major cause of the Revolution, he was also aware of the financial crisis of the French monarchy long before it reached its climax in 1788–89. Also, he did not ignore the economic origins of the Revolution, including the agricultural disasters in France during 1788 and 1789. In the *Annual Register* for 1789 there is an account of two natural calamities—a dreadful hurricane which destroyed the harvest and vineyards in several of the finest provinces of the kingdom, and two successive failures of crops. Burke also knew that the distresses of the French people were greatly increased during the severity of the winter of 1788. These sorts of occasional catastrophes can create anxiety and suffering, but they are not causes of revolution so much as the precipitating occasions. The growing debt of the monarchy was of much greater importance in bringing about the Revolution. As early as 1769 Burke predicted that France was headed for very serious trouble. In a speech in Parliament he noted that the debt of France was growing larger and larger and he predicted that the explosion that would come would rack France and possibly all of Europe to its foundations. In helping the Americans in their rebellion against Britain, France increased its debt by $170 million. This precipitated the financial crisis that compelled the King to convene the Estates-General in May 1789.

Certainly no revolution ever started with higher expectations than the French Revolution, nor degenerated so quickly into anarchy, violence, terror, collective tyranny, and the civil and foreign wars that the Revolution provoked. By far the most important early step taken by the revolutionists at Versailles was noted by Burke in the *Reflections*, an action filled with implications of a very radical change in the structure of the French government and French society:

> In the calling of Estates-General of France, the first thing that struck me was a great departure from the ancient course. I found the representation for the Third Estate composed of six hundred persons. They were equal in number to the representatives of both of the other orders. If the orders were to act separately, that is corporately, the number would not, beyond the consideration of expense, be of much moment. But when it became apparent that the three orders were to be melted down into one, the policy and necessary effect of this numerous representation in the Third Estate became obvious. A very small desertion from either of the other two orders must throw the power of both into the hands of the third. In fact, the whole power of the state was soon resolved into that body. Its due composition became, therefore, of infinitely the greater importance.

In the composition of the representatives to the Estates-General, Burke noted, a great many of them had no political experience whatsoever; they were wholly unqualified to restructure the French government and society. This fact, plus the rejection of the British model of a limited constitutional monarchy with two legislative branches, in favor of a unicameral form of government, with no checks or balances to prevent any dominant faction from securing absolute arbitrary power, determined the whole direction the Revolution was to follow.

Many scholars have remarked on Burke's power of prophecy regarding the French Revolution, and truly his insights are almost incredible. He predicted a revolution long before it occurred. His firsthand knowledge of France came in 1773, when he visited Paris and placed his son with a provincial family so that he could learn French.

During this month-long visit, Burke made the rounds of French society: he visited the prime minister; he kissed the King's hand; he saw Marie Antoinette from a distance; he visited Versailles and attended the salons in Paris, where he heard the talk of the free-thinking deists and atheists among the *philosophes*. In his first speech on returning to England he had to deal with the claims of the Protestant dissenters of England for lifting certain of their civil disabilities. Burke was wholly in favor of extending constitutional rights to the Dissenters, so far as it was consistent with the safety of the realm and did not threaten the Church of England. But he took occasion to warn his colleagues in the House of Commons of the dangers of atheism that he had perceived in France. He warned that atheists in political power would strip away the moral clothing that the institutions of society provided, and would leave no toleration to any religion. He stated: "The most horrid and cruel blow that can be offered to civil society is through atheism." Twenty-three years later, in his second *Letters on a Regicide Peace*, Burke wrote: "This fanatical atheism left out, we omit the principal feature in the French Revolution." Burke always regarded the Jacobin faction in the National Assembly as usurpers, "a college of armed fanatics," who had seized absolute arbitrary power over the French people: they were not the true representatives of France. In their efforts to spread their revolution to all of Europe through war, Burke denied that they represented France:

> It is a war between the partisans of the ancient, civil, moral, and political order of Europe, against a sect of fanatical and ambitious atheists which means to change them all. It is not France extending a foreign empire over other nations; it is a sect aiming at universal empire, and beginning with the conquest of France.

Many of Burke's accurate predictions on the course of the French Revolution can be traced to his conviction that its essential character was its fanatical atheism.

Burke well understood Dostoevski's famous remark that without God all things are permissible, including the massacres and violence of the French Revolution, which Burke predicted. He prophesied the executions of the King and Queen; the Reign of Terror; the fall to worthlessness of the paper currency, the *assignats;* the wars of aggression by the revolutionists in attempting to export their revolution to all of Europe; the triumph of Napoleon and the long series of wars over many years. Every one of Burke's predictions turned out to be true. At the time that he charted the course of the Revolution, many of his peers in the British government considered him something of a madman, because they were convinced that the Revolution was the prelude to a glorious future for all of humanity. Even after Burke's words were verified by events, many of his contemporaries, including Charles James Fox and Richard B. Sheridan and other leaders of his party, never publicly retracted their errors. So far as I know, nobody has ever accused such enthusiasts for the Revolution of being insane, which may signify that revolutionary ideology is more real to its adherents than the facts of history.

Let us now turn to Rousseau and consider his view of history, the nature and function of civil institutions, and his conception of the moral nature of man. Madame de Staël, the daughter of Necker, once remarked that Rousseau originated nothing but he set everything aflame. There is considerable truth in her statement. The paradoxes in Rousseau's writings certainly created much agitation in the intellectual life of Europe, and in that sense did set everything aflame. In 1750, in his *Discourse on the Arts and Sciences*, Rousseau clearly put forth a revolutionary thesis regarding history and civilization. That work is a strong condemnation of the historically developed social institutions of Europe. In effect, Rousseau said

56

that man comes from the hands of his creator in a pure state, that he is born morally good, but becomes corrupted in the process of living in organized society. Like Hobbes and Locke before him, Rousseau began by positing a belief in a supposed pre-civil "state of nature," before organized society existed, but his fictional state of nature was much more idyllic than that of Locke, and totally contrary to the jungle that Hobbes had imagined it to be. Rousseau's state of nature was like a Garden of Eden, in which mankind lived in innocence in a "natural society," without institutions or laws, in a state of perfect equality. In this happy state men possessed "natural rights," but upon creating artificial society through a "social contract" these natural rights were warped or lost, and men became enslaved to the institutions of artificial society.

Nothing could be further from Burke's view that "art is man's nature," and that the institutions of man were the necessary and good instruments of his fulfillment in civil society. The great differences between Burke and Rousseau are clearly evident in their views of "natural rights." Rousseau believed that the original "natural rights" of man in a state of nature provided the norm for men in civil society, a concept assumed by the radical revolutionaries in France. Burke considered these so-called "natural rights" a violation of the true "natural rights" of men derived from the moral natural law. According to Burke, the true "natural rights" of men are to be found within the historical order of civilization, and the attempt to fulfill the supposed "rights of man" in a pre-historical state among men in historical society would destroy civilization. In the *Reflections* he wrote: "Men cannot enjoy the rights of an uncivil and of a civil state together." And again: "Far am I from denying in theory, full as far is my heart from withholding in practice, (if I were of power to give or to withhold,) the real rights of men. In denying their false claims of right, I do not mean to injure those which are real, and are such as their pretended rights would totally destroy." Any attempt to apply the supposed ideal norms of a state of nature to organized society would in effect wipe out all that has been achieved through history, and create a *tabula rasa:* "I cannot conceive how any man can have brought himself to that pitch of presumption to consider his country as nothing but carteblanche upon which he may scribble whatever he pleases." Although Rousseau himself explicitly denied the possibility of any return to a state of nature, one possible logical result of his thesis in his *Discourse on the Arts and Sciences* was to destroy the historically developed society of Europe which he had condemned.

The basic thrust in Rousseau's second important work, *A Discourse on the Origin of Inequality* (1755), is an attack on private property as the cause of inequality and injustices among men:

> The first man, who, having enclosed a piece of ground, bethought himself of saying "this is mine"— and found people simple enough to believe him—was the real founder of civil society. From how many crimes, wars, and murders, from how many horrors and misfortunes, might not anyone have saved mankind by pulling up the stakes or filling up the ditch and crying to his fellows "beware of listening to this imposter. You are undone if you once forget that the fruits of the earth belong to us all and the earth to nobody."

In the pre-civil state of nature nobody owned property, and if that was to be the norm for men in organized society, as the basis for justice between men, then all property should be collectivized and owned by the state. Rousseau's argument clearly implied that all the major conflicts in civil society were the result of some men aggrandizing to themselves what morally belonged equally to everyone. In this principle Rousseau stated the Marxist economic theory of property in a nutshell. The theory implied that there was a necessary antithesis between wealth and poverty, a class war that assumes the economic pie is static, so that if anyone has more than he needs he has taken it from someone else who needs it but has been robbed of it. That Rousseau believed this is evident in his statements that the wealth of the rich is the cause of the poverty of the poor. In total contrast with Rousseau, Burke held that wealth is an expandable matter, that it is not limited, and that no cause and effect relationship exists between wealth and poverty.

The logical consequence of combining Rousseau's "state of nature" when all men were equal, and his theory that private property is the cause of inequality and injustice, is most evident during the French Revolution in the actions of Marat and Babeuf. Lord Acton, in his *Lectures on the French Revolution* (1920), summarized the character and theory of Marat as follows:

> Marat . . . who demanded not only slaughter but torture, and whose ferocity was revolting and grotesque, even Marat was obedient to a logic of his own. He adopted simply the state of nature and the primitive contract, in which thousands of his contemporaries believed. The poor had agreed to renounce the rights of savage life and the prerogative of force, in return for the benefits of civilisation; but finding the compact broken on the other side, finding that the upper classes governed in their own interest, and left them to misery and ignorance, they resumed the conditions of barbaric existence before society, and were free to take what they required, and to inflict what punishment they chose upon men who had made a profit of their sufferings.

By appealing to "the rights of man" in a state of nature, the wholesale confiscation of private and corporate property and the slaughter of nobles, priests, wealthy peasants, and businessmen, was not only justified but was a revolutionary necessity and virtue. Babeuf, the first Communist revolutionary, made the same argument as Marat—that in confiscating property the revolutionaries were simply taking back what was rightfully theirs, which they had been deprived of for centuries. Burke commented on this theory of the Revolution as follows, in his *Letter to a Noble Lord:*

> The learned professors of the Rights of Man regard prescription not as a title to bar all claim set up against old possession, but they look on prescription as itself a bar against the possessor and proprietor. They hold an immemorial possession to be no more than a long continued and therefore aggravated injustice.

Thus, in the name of the French nation as a whole, the Jacobins systematically confiscated whatever private and institutional property they wished to possess, and added moral indignation against those whom they robbed.

In Rousseau's third important work, *A Discourse on Political Economy* (1755), which first appeared in Volume V of the *Encyclopédie* of Diderot and D'Alembert, he denied that the natural identity of interests which prevails between a father and his family applies to a ruler and his relationship to his subjects in society. Rousseau insisted that between the will of the sovereign and the needs, rights, and desires of citizens there was a sharp antithesis which needed to be overcome before government could rule over a just society. His emphasis on the self-interest of rulers as opposed to the interests of subjects is potentially a revolutionary principle. In this work for the first time Rousseau uses the term "general will," which he defines as that which "tends always to the preservation and welfare of the whole and of every part and is the source of the laws." He notes that between the parts and the whole of society there is an inevitable conflict of interests which divides the state, because the particular wills and interests of the many "smaller societies" or corporate bodies prevent unity of the whole nation.

Rousseau then argues for the absolute sovereignty of the "legislator," a law-giver whose first duty is to make the laws conform to the "general will." How is this to be done? According to Rousseau, "If you would have the general will accomplished, bring all the particular wills into conformity with it . . . as virtue is nothing more than this conformity of the particular wills with the general will, establish the reign of virtue." To ensure the long-range conformity of citizens to the general will of the state, Rousseau advocates that the state, rather than parents, should prescribe the education of children. In his *A Discourse on the Origin of Inequality* he had attacked private property, but in *A Discourse on Political Economy* he defends it, including the right of inheritance. On this important point, as in many others, Rousseau can be found on both sides of every issue, which is why it is next to impossible to generalize about his philosophy without being contradicted. Having defended property rights, he concludes this work by attacking the presumed social contract between rich and poor as wholly unjust to the poor, and advocates taxing out of existence all luxuries, useless public entertainments, and the arts.

Rousseau's *Social Contract* (1762) is much too complex to analyze here; it is a long, speculative, abstract treatise on society and government, on the order of Plato's *Republic*, Hobbes' *Leviathan*, and Locke's two treatises. His central thesis emerges as the concept of the sovereignty of "the people" as an expression of the "general will." In *A Discourse on Popular Economy* Rousseau had claimed that the "general will" (a phrase he probably borrowed from Diderot) contradicts the "social contract." But in the *Social Contract* he attempts to reconcile these two concepts and to harmonize them with primitive "natural rights." He abandons his assertion in the earlier work that the majority will spoke for the "general will," and sets forth a theory of the "general will" that makes it appear closer to traditional moral natural law. Among Rousseau scholars the range of interpretations of what he meant by the "general will" is almost as great as the number of scholars. Certainly there is no consensus, except perhaps the negative consensus that he did not mean a mere majority will.

In the *Social Contract* political sovereignty in the state involves much more than an expression of the people's majority will. Rousseau makes no clear distinction between sovereignty which originates in "the people," and then is transmitted to others through their representatives in government, and sovereignty directly expressed by the people at large, without representatives as intermediaries. He took ancient Sparta and modern Geneva as his political models, and argued in favor of direct democracy, so that his theory of a free government precluded a representative republic such as the American. He expressly denied that direct participatory democracy was feasible for a large nation, an injunction which his disciples completely ignored during the French Revolution.

Rousseau's conception of "the people" was centered in numbers, not as with Burke in the corporate nature of man in his institutions. Isolated individuals counted by the head, as in a state of nature, in their collective totality in civil society constituted "the people." Thus the voice of "the people" was to Rousseau as the voice of God, an infallible imperative, and therefore incapable of tyranny. Burke also venerated "the people," not merely as a numerous, undifferentiated multitude without moral or legal leadership, but as incorporated into their social institutions. In rejecting Rousseau's theory of numbers as infallible, Burke once remarked that the tyranny of a multitude is a multiple tyranny. There is no assurance that the inherent rights to life, liberty, and property will not be violated simply because a vast multitude of individuals is involved in making or authorizing political decisions.

One of Rousseau's chief disciples in the Estates-General, the Abbé Sieyès, adopted his conception of "the people," and in his famous pamphlet, *Qu' est-ce que le tiers etat?* (January 1789), he answered that the Third Estate is everything, that it has long been nothing, and that it demands to become something. Sieyès held that the first two orders, the nobility and the clergy, were usurpers and even criminals, and when he convinced the delegates in the merged orders to call themselves the "National Assembly," he effectively excluded the King, the nobility, and the clergy from having any important role in reforming France through its traditional corporate orders. Lord Acton considered Sieyès "the most perfect representative of the Revolution," and noted that his influence in the Estates-General was decisive in determining the early course of the Revolution: "Within a fortnight of his maiden speech he had vanquished the ancient order of things in France. The Court, the Church, and the *Noblesse* had gone down before the imposing coherence of his ideas."

Also, in pursuit of Rousseau's principle that the "general will" had to eliminate or absorb the various "particular wills" into a social unity, Sieyès destroyed the traditional provinces of France, and converted them into geometrically equalized "departments." Thus the Revolution destroyed the provincial and local community life of France and replaced it with a national collectivism. Burke satirized Sieyès for this action, and also portrayed him as a metaphysically insane constitution-monger whose paper constitutions violated the historical inheritance of France.

As a severe critic of the Old Regime, Rousseau should not be identified with the *philosophes*, such as Voltaire, who despised him, or with Diderot, who began as his friend but in time became alienated from him. The *philosophes* were deists or atheists, and had an unbounded faith in the power of their reason as a trustworthy instrument for arriving at truth. In contrast, Rousseau was a theist for many years, and later a pantheist, and in Part One of the *Social Contract* he set forth a famous anti-rationalist paradoxical aphorism: "A man who meditates is a depraved animal." Rousseau (and to some extent Diderot) was essentially a man of sensibility. He distrusted discursive reason and logic and the methods of science, and placed his faith in his emotions, intuition, and imagination as higher instruments for knowing truth. His acceptance of a pre-civil state of nature made him something of a primitivist (depending on how that ambiguous term is defined), a concept that called forth contempt from Voltaire. In politics Voltaire and his colleagues were oligarchs, and deeply distrusted the masses in whom Rousseau placed such faith.

In Book IV, Chapter 8 of Rousseau's *Social Contract,* called "Civil Religion," he advances the theory that the Church should be, in effect, a department of the state. He very much approves of Thomas Hobbes' thesis on this subject in the *Leviathan:* both men reduce religion to mere patriotism. One paragraph from Rousseau's "Civil Religion" reads as follows:

> There is, therefore, a purely civil profession of faith of which the sovereign should fix the articles. Not exactly as religious dogmas but as social sentiments without which a man can not be a good citizen or a faithful subject. While it can compel no one to believe them, it can banish from the state whoever does not believe them. It can banish him not for impiety but as an anti-social being incapable of truly loving the laws of justice and of sacrificing at need his life to his duty.

As if his civil religion were not tyrannical enough, Rousseau follows this statement with a sentence which almost leaps out of the page:

> If anyone after publicly recognizing these dogmas behaves as if he does not believe them let him be punished by death. He has committed the worst of all crimes—that of lying before the law.

Most Rousseau admirers are embarrassed by this paragraph, because it clearly advocates religious persecution in order to achieve unity in the "general will." His civil religion, or patriotism, in effect holds that politicians in government, exercising sovereignty for "the people," have the right and even the duty to exile or put to death anyone they decide is insufficiently patriotic.

State-Church relations under the first constitution of the Revolution moved rapidly: from August 1789 when religious orders were suppressed, (and in a few years nine orders were abolished), to November 1789 when the National Assembly confiscated all Church property, to the Civil Constitution of the Clergy in July 1790, which established a national church independent from Rome, on principles very similar to Rousseau's civil profession of faith. Thousands of non-juring priests refused to conform, and were driven into exile, or went underground, or were imprisoned and executed. Ironically, the very attempt by the revolutionists to create unity through a national church which excluded Roman Catholicism, the religion of the great majority of the French people, divided the nation and resulted in a strong counterrevolutionary movement which ultimately prevailed over the Revolution. Of course, the anticlerical revolutionists did not need to appeal to Rousseau to persecute Christianity, but it is significant that their persecution of the clergy, on the grounds they were not loyal citizens of the new revolu-

tionary order, is identical with the central principle in Rousseau's civil profession of faith. The protection of individual "natural rights" proclaimed by the Revolution was violated against both laity and clergy, by appeals to the "general will" of "the people" through the absolute power of the unicameral National Assembly. In his political theory in the *Social Contract* Rousseau had not been able to solve this conflict, and in practice the National Assembly revealed that there was no way to reconcile these contradictory revolutionary principles.

Perhaps the most radical theory in Rousseau's *Social Contract* is in Book II, Chapter 7, called "The Legislator," in which he empowers his lawgiver to regenerate the moral nature of man:

> He who dares to undertake the making of a people's institutions ought to feel himself capable, so to speak, of changing human nature, of transforming each individual, who is by himself a complete and solitary whole, into part of a greater whole from which he in a manner receives his life and being; of altering man's constitution for the purpose of strengthening it; and of substituting a partial and moral existence for the physical and independent existence nature has conferred on us all. He must, in a word, take away from man his own resources and give him instead new ones alien to him, and incapable of being made use of without the help of other men. The more completely these natural resources are annihilated, the greater and more lasting are those which he acquires, and the more stable and perfect the new institutions; so that if each citizen is nothing and can do nothing without the rest, and the resources acquired by the whole are equal or superior to the aggregate of the resources of all the individuals, it may be said that legislation is at the highest possible point of perfection.

Rousseau's legislator, whose "genius" and "office" is "an individual and superior function" in the state, above the constitution, would have the power and right to destroy the whole character of each individual, as he exists in the corrupt or imperfect state of traditional civil society, in order to regenerate his moral nature by making him "into part of the greater whole" of the collective revolutionary society. This implies that each individual human being is mere raw material to be shaped by the state into virtue, so that the republic of virtue can achieve "more stable and perfect . . . new institutions." Rousseau's law-giving legislator is clearly the archetype for every modern dictator in a totalitarian system of government. The claim that his lawgiver is benevolent changes nothing on this vital point.

The epiphany which Rousseau had experienced in the summer of 1749 on the road to Vincennes, so graphically described in Book VIII of his *Confessions*, which convinced him that "man is naturally good" and becomes corrupted by his institutions, reached its culmination in practical politics in his chief revolutionary disciple, Maximilien Robespierre. Several revolutionaries, including Marat, conceived of themselves as lawgivers to the new revolutionary order, but as leader of the Jacobins in the Paris Commune Robespierre's entire political career was consciously devoted to establishing a republic of virtue on Rousseau's principles. Three recent studies have explored this subject in great and various detail: Norman Hampson, *Will and Circumstances: Montesquieu, Rousseau, and the French Revolution* (1983); James Miller, *Rousseau: Dreamer of Democracy* (1984); and Carol Blum, *Rousseau and the Republic of Virtue* (1986). These works of scholarship effectively refute several studies, such as Joan McDonald's *Rousseau and the French Revolution: 1762–1791* (1965), which have denied that Rousseau had any notable influence on the French Revolution. These three studies present conclusive evidence that the moral justification for Robespierre's Reign of Terror derives from his conviction that human nature must be morally regenerated from the corruptions in men from the historical inheritance of the Old Regime, into the republican virtues of a wholly new society.

Recent studies which have noted the great importance of Rousseau in influencing the politics of the Revolution seem to confirm Burke's savage criticism of Rousseau in his *A Letter to a Member of the National Assembly* (1791). Burke castigates Rousseau for about nine pages in some of the harshest criticism ever written against him, and after describing some of the worst features of the Revolution he writes: "I am certain that the writings of Rousseau lead directly to this kind of shameful evil." Burke's conviction that the rationalism of the *philosophes*, and the ethics of feeling in Rousseau's sensibility, were among the chief causes of the French Revolution, dominated interpretations of the Revolution during much of the nineteenth century, and even down to the present it has its adherents. Long before 1789 Burke believed that the accumulations of strong animosity against the Church, the Crown, the nobility, and the whole historical inheritance of France, in the generation that was taught by Mercier de la Rivière, Mably, Morelly, Meslier, Turgot, Helvétius, the Abbé Raynal, Holbach, D'Alembert, Diderot, Melchior Grimm, and especially Voltaire and Rousseau, would eventually converge and bear fruit in the revolutionary thinking and actions of such men as Mirabeau, Condorcet, the Abbé Sieyès, Danton, Marat, Brissot de Warville, Camille Desmoulins, Anarcharsis Cloots, Jacques Hébert, Bertrand Barère, Saint-Just, and Robespierre.

But the assumed intellectual causes of the French Revolution have been largely replaced by economic, social, and political interpretations of the Revolution, so that among modern liberal academic historians Burke's interpretation is no longer considered tenable. It is next to impossible to prove a direct cause and effect connection between the ideas of any writer during the 1740s and post-mid-century and specific political events after 1789. More than a dozen of the chief revolutionaries claimed that they were disciples or admirers of Rousseau, but scholars have pointed out that this means nothing, because many of them were simply riding the wave of the popularity of Rousseau, and had not even read him, or did not really understand him. There is ample evidence that the Abbé Sieyès and Robespierre did read and understand Rousseau very well. To complicate matters further, anti-revolutionary French conservatives also appealed to Rousseau in opposing specific measures of the revolutionists.

Carol Blum, in the preface to *Rousseau and the Republic of Virtue*, describes the scholarly swings of the pendulum in the interpretations of the supposed causes of the French Revolution, from the intellectual to the economic, political, and social factors. She notes that J. L. Talmon and Lester Crocker

> both . . . found blueprints for modern totalitarian societies in the writing of eighteenth-century thinkers, especially Rousseau. *This* reading, in turn, provoked reactions of dismay both from liberal admirers of Rousseau, indignant that he was being blamed for events and patterns of behavior which he had never imagined, and from Marxists, who objected to the word and the concept "totalitarian". . . . Between the two poles, however, between the affirmation that Rousseau and some other eighteenth-century thinkers had somehow provided a model for the Revolution, the Terror, and subsequent manifestations of totalitarianism, and the denial of any connection between literature and events, the distance has begun to close.

But bridging the distance between the revolutionary ideas in literature in the generation before the Revolution, and the practical politics of revolutionaries after 1789, is perhaps less feasible and less significant than determining the extent to which the culture of the Old Regime was effectively destroyed by the rationalism and moral sensibility of writers during the Enlightenment, which prepared the way for the Revolution. In the case of Rousseau, for this complex enterprise, scholars would need to study his two novels, *La Nouvelle Heloise* (1761); *Emile* (1762); and *The Confessions of Jean-Jacques Rousseau* (1782 and 1789), more than his political and social writings. All three of these works contain ideas that are potentially or actually revolutionary, in society more than in political theory. Perhaps the dominant image which runs through all three works is that of the virtuous individual, filled with natural goodness, Romantic sensibility, and an intense love of simple "Nature," suffering injustices and indignities from depraved men in power in a corrupt society. Burke's remark that "Rousseau is a moralist or he is nothing" would take on enormous significance from such a study, both for an understanding of Rousseau and his real or supposed role in the French Revolution.

THE AGE OF
THE GUILLOTINE
(Sade, Robespierre, and the Consequences)

ERIK RITTER VON KUEHNELT-LEDDIHN

Erik Ritter von Kuehnelt-Leddihn is a well-known writer, artist, and philosopher. Born in Austria, he studied at the University of Vienna, the Theological School of Vienna University, and the University of Budapest where he was awarded his Ph.D. In America, he has taught at Georgetown University, St. Peter's College, Fordham University, and Chestnut Hill College. He has innumerable theoretical books and articles for national and international publications to his credit. Of the many novels he has written, Gates of Hell, Moscow 1979, Black Banners, *and* Die Gottlosen, *or* The Godless Ones, *have received considerable attention. His nonfiction works include:* Liberty or Equality?, Catholicism in America, America's Founding Fathers, Seeds of Anarchy, *and* Leftism: From Sade and Marx to Hitler and Pol Pot *(Regnery Gateway 1990).*

> The absolute ruler can be a Nero,
> but at times he can be a Titus or a Marcus Aurelius,
> the people is sometimes a Nero,
> but never a Marcus Aurelius.
> —*Rivarol*

I N THE SUMMER of 1989 the bicentenary of the French Revolution was celebrated in a festival costing millions

71

and millions of dollars—but care was taken not to feature too many details of that evil event. Already in the 1880s, long after the last eyewitnesses of the storming of the Bastille had died, one began to commemorate this gruesome episode of French history with music, dancing, and fireworks. Leftist historians tried to present the French Revolution in an idyllic light, but in recent years attempts have been made to reveal its true nature.

The early phase of the French Revolution had a somewhat elitist character. The ideas of the First Enlightenment had, at first, influenced only the top layers of society. This was a period of financial crisis in the public sector and prosperity in the private sector, coupled with the beginnings of far-reaching reforms. Rousseau's sentimental foolishness, the anti-religious and anti-semitic writings of Voltaire (who had only contempt for the common people), as well as the perpetual strife between the Jansenists and the official Church, disrupted the uppermost social layers. Also not to be underestimated is the part played by Benjamin Franklin (so brilliantly analyzed by D. H. Lawrence) as well as by Freemasonry; even Louis XVI might have been a member of the *Frères*. (He was an enthusiastic reader of the *Encyclopédie*.) A religious and moral vacuum meant that leftist ideologies seeped downward into ever broader layers. A leftist *intelligentsia*, together with the fashionable set, laid the foundations for the Revolution, although, in the beginning, the monarchy was attacked only with a certain reserve, and the hierarchy put up hardly any resistance—too many parlor abbés had lost their faith a long time ago.

The most alarming danger signal in this process of disintegration, however, was not the fraternization between the Estates in the *Jeu de Paume*, but the storming of the Bastille, a luxurious jail reserved for the nobility. In this, one man played a part at least as important as that of Rousseau: the Marquis de Sade, after whom sadism is named. His numerous and rather boring pornographic essays contain long philosophic, political, and anti-religious tirades and, in a way, he instigated the storming of the Bastille. Upon his mother-in-law's request he was imprisoned there, together with a few card sharpers, money forgers, and other similar crooks. Through a funnel, which he used as a megaphone, he appealed through the grilled window for the liberation of "innocent prisoners." The governor of the Bastille submitted a petition to the King, asking for the removal of this highly inconvenient prisoner, who was thereupon transferred on July 4, 1789, to the hospital for the criminally insane in Charenton. Dismissed from there in 1791, the now fanatically Jacobin "citizen Brutus Sade" became chief of the revolutionary *Section des Piques.* But he soon quarrelled with Robespierre, was imprisoned once more, and, after the fall of Robespierre, was sent back to Charenton. Together with Rousseau, a self-confessed masochist who wrote volumes full of pedagogical theories but put his own children into orphanages, Sade is a hero of the European left. Ten days after his removal from the Bastille his appeals bore fruit. The prison surrendered to the raging mob and a ghastly massacre followed.

The "storming" and its consequences highlight the French Revolution—a moral breakdown prepared by leftist ideas. De Launay, the commander of the Bastille, had achieved a promise of safe conduct for the small garrison consisting of Swiss mercenaries and a few *invalides.* But as soon as these men left the fortress they were brutally killed, the *invalides* literally chopped up. De Launay's head did not come off easily and a butcher's apprentice, *qui savait faire les viandes,* had to be found, who managed to cut off the head which was then carried triumphantly through the streets of Paris.

There was an attempt to transform the absolute monarchy into a constitutional one, but once the tide had set in, it could not be stopped. Goethe was probably right when he wrote: "Had the kings been kings, they would still stand today." The egalitarian passions were heading for a climax. The words of Benjamin Constant come to mind: "In certain epochs one must run the whole cycle of madness in order to return to reason." And don't let us deceive ourselves: The cycle is not yet completely closed.

It was Robespierre's fall that prevented further "reforms." "The Pure One" had envisaged not only uniforms for every Frenchman and Frenchwoman (remember Mao's "Blue Ants"), he also made plans to destroy all church towers because they were "undemocratic." Another problem were the Alsatians *qui ne parlaient pas la langue républicaine,* who did not speak French. Some Jacobins proposed that their children and those of the German-speaking Lorrainers should be confiscated, while others suggested that the two populations should be scattered all over France. But the most "practical" solution, proposed by a few fanatics, was their total extermination. As one can see, the French Revolution was the overture to the "Age of the G," of guillotines, gaols, gallows, the Gestapo, gas chambers, and gulags. The guillotine marks the first step toward a mechanical-technological mass extermination, toward genocide. The *République une et indivisible,* the one and indivisible republic, should be all of one piece, a nation of faceless, undifferentiated masses.

Materialists of all shades like to regard the French Revolution as a reaction to adverse circumstances, to calamities, particularly those of an economic or social nature, and to a corrupt class system. Foreigners who visited France, on the other hand—such as Burke and Young from Britain, or Benjamin Rush, one of the Founding Fathers, from the United States—were full of praise for the nobility, the clergy, and the *grande bourgeoisie.* The real weakness of the *ancien régime* lay in the skepticism, godlessness, and envy propagated by the First Enlightenment, especially—as we said before—in the uppermost circles. It was a case of human "titanism"—a belief that the city of God should be replaced by the city of man.

It would be difficult to explain the horrors committed since 1792 in any other manner. There was the ghoulish slaughtering of the Princesse de Lamballe, an intimate friend of the Queen. This frivolous lady had courageously refused to give the oath on the constitution, whereupon she was brutally killed, eviscerated like an animal and her private parts made into an "arrangement" which was carried in triumph to the Tuileries to be shown to Marie Antoinette. This crime opened the series of "September Massacres" instigated by the "moderate republican" Danton. The killers were given quantities of wine and six *livres* a day for their services. Most of the prisons were emptied through mass killings in which not only political prisoners, but also prostitutes and juvenile delinquents, some of them mere children, were sacrificed to the "republican virtues." What was done at the time in the name of democratization recalls Goya's *desastres de la guerra.* The most horrible scenes took place in the Bicêtre and Salpetriere prisons. (In the Spanish Civil War the Republicans, so much admired by our leftists, also killed prostitutes because they infected the brave warriors for democracy with all sorts of unpleasant diseases.) In the same year the Tuileries, too, were stormed, although the Swiss Guards, faithful to their oath, fought to the last man. (The lion carved in stone in the city of Lucerne is dedicated to their memory.) Whoever of these "mercenaries" fell into the hands of the mob alive was tortured to death. A young cook's apprentice who had tried to defend his king was wrapped in butter and roasted alive.

In quantity, the crimes of the Red and Brown Socialists surpass those of the French Revolution, but in quality, that is to say, morally, these were far worse. The former perpetrated their horrors mostly in closed concentration camps, prisons, or underground places through dehumanized "special units." Those of the French Revolution, however, were committed in the name of liberty, equality, and fraternity, by the dear people, in broad daylight, before

75

a frantically applauding mob. *La terreur* held no mysteries and was merely intended to spread paralyzing fear. Later, the murderous monsters of the Revolution were treated very humanely and nearly all of them eventually led normal lives . . . even some of the *regicides*, the king's assassins, returned in 1830 under Louis Philippe.

But all this was only the beginning. Beheadings became a favorite amusement for the crowds—like the executions in Guinea under Sékou Touré, or in Equatorial Africa under Macias Nguema, who crucified Christian opponents. I shall cite only one example in the French case: an old man, strapped to the guillotine, was read a long list of republican victories at the front, with the idea that he would report them to his ancestors in the next world. It took a long time until the falling axe put an end to his suffering. But not only the nobility was brought to *notre chère mère, la guillotine.* Soon wealth alone sufficed as a reason. Actually only eight percent of those formally condemned to the guillotine belonged to the nobility; more than 30 percent were farmers. The fate of the "moderates" was not much better. Lyon, Toulon, and Bordeaux, cities which had revolted against the radical Jacobins, were laid waste, and thousands upon thousands of their inhabitants butchered. Whenever the guillotine did not work fast enough, the dissidents were drowned en masse or mowed down with guns. (Napoleon, at that time a Jacobin and close friend of Robespierre's brother Augustin, was "the slaughterer of Toulon," the city that had in vain expected help from England.)

The French "democrats" depopulated whole areas with diabolic thoroughness, often involving the satisfaction of nearly all varieties of sexual perversion. Saint-Just's declaration (October 10, 1793) that not only "traitors" but "indifferents" too, should be done away with, was a driving factor. Others like Danton declared that aristocrats and priests, by their very existence, constituted a threat to the republic. Robespierre demanded quick, severe, and inflexible justice as a dictate of virtue and consequence of the democratic principle. This principle was applied in the Vendée where a peasant rebellion was joined by the nobility and clergy. What was done there can be gleaned from the report of General Westermann to the Welfare Committee:

> The Vendée is no more, my republican comrades! With her women and children she died under our sabres. I have just buried them in the swamps and forests. As you ordered, the children were trampled to death by our horses, the women butchered so that they no longer can give birth to little brigands. The streets are littered with corpses which sometimes are stacked in pyramids. Mass shootings are taking place in Savenay because there brigands keep turning up to surrender. We do not take any prisoners because they would have to be fed the bread of freedom, but pity is incompatible with the spirit of revolution.

Westermann, however, soon got his just reward; he and Carrier were guillotined together with their good friend Danton. All leftist revolutions eventually devour their children.

Apocalyptic scenes occurred in Le Mans. Women, children, and old people in hiding were hunted down while their men fought against the Republic. The leaders of that hunt were Barbotte and Prieur. Having found their victims, they violated and murdered the girls and women, and since there were not enough live females to satisfy their libido, necrophile orgies were celebrated. Following the example of Arras, "National batteries" were built with the naked corpses. In Angers the hanged were decapitated, the heads prepared by doctors and impaled on the battlements. Since the number of "politicals" was not sufficient, jailbirds and mere suspects were added.

Hell-Breughel and Hieronymus Bosch could have done

pictorial justice to the horrors committed in the hospitals of Avranche and Fougère (Normandy), where female relatives of the *Chouans* were raped and slowly tortured to death. It gave the soldiers a satanic pleasure to explode gunpowder in their vaginas—a "game" played also by the Spanish Loyalists in Andalusia.

The "Blues," those valiant warriors of the *colonnes infernales*, also enjoyed baking women and children alive. To heighten this pleasure, the victims were put into cold ovens so that the procedure was protracted. General Margeau-Desvallier, who had no sympathy with that kind of humor but who did not succeed in restraining his "freedom-loving" men, became melancholic. He had the good fortune to be killed in battle fighting against the Austrians soon thereafter in 1796. Of General Turreau's men it is said that they were worse than cannibals, but all they did was to execute his orders when they burned down houses and erected *batteries nationales*. The general later made a great career: from 1803 to 1811 he was Napoleon's Ambassador to the United States (where he helped to shape the French-American Alliance against Britain) and his sculptured effigy can be seen on the east side of the Arc de Triomphe.

The Girondistes were not much better than the Jacobins. The former Girondiste Barrere declared that he would transform the Vendée into a graveyard. Since the men of the Vendée were fighting against the Revolution, their women and children had to do penance. (In principle, though not in detail, the British used the same method in the Boer War when they put up concentration camps for the families of the Boer guerilla fighters.) In the Vendée, the "Blues" threw children from windows to their comrades below who caught them on their bayonets. Pregnant women were cut open, their fetuses chopped up and the women left to die a slow and painful death. They were also squashed in wine or fruit presses. Many were killed in the burning of houses and churches. The bloodthirst knew

78

no bounds. Finally, Commander Grignon ordered all Ven-
déens to be killed, even those who were loyal to the Republic. The soldiers lacked many qualities, but certainly
not imagination. As a last of the endless list of horrors, let
me cite one more example: a young girl, naked and raped,
was hung, head down, with her legs tied to the branches of
two trees, and slit open like a butchered animal.

The Jacobins, as brave materialists, also thought to
make good use of their dead victims. Of their hair they
made wigs or fillings for mattresses, and their skins were
made into leather for aprons, riding breeches, and book
bindings. (Male skin was found to be superior in quality.)
Grease was also extracted from some corpses. The former
Abbé Morellet even proposed to establish "national butch-
eries" in which the flesh of executed "reactionaries"
would be sold, especially on national holidays in the form
of a "Republican Eucharist."

The harm brought to France and then to all of Europe,
the human and cultural destruction wrought by these
Vandals is all but immeasurable. The devastated interiors
of many French churches and cathedrals still bear witness
to the ideas of the "progressive" mob.

Did the French Revolution leave us anything positive?
Only the metric system, a very apt legacy, since democracy is principally preoccupied with numbers and measures. Obligatory military service, ethnic nationalism,
and class hatred, on the other hand, were barbed gifts.
Simple minds might regard the *Declaration des droits de
l'Homme et du Citoyen,* conceived in 1789 and incorporated in 1793 into the constitution of a sadistic murderers'
republic, as a positive contribution, whereas it only shows
what somersaults a godless humanism can perform.
About the Terror one can read in French schoolbooks: *La
Terreur était terrible, mais grande.* That many so-called
"moderates" like Danton were among its victims can be
called tragic justice since they had not taken into consideration the fact that it is always very risky to destroy an

existing order. (Kerenski was reproached for this by Kat-kov.) Charlotte Corday d'Armont, a Girondiste, finally killed Marat. André Chenier, the great liberal poet, was beheaded shortly before Robespierre fell, the Marquis de Condorcet, whose philosophy the "moderates" had adopted, committed suicide in order to evade the "na-tional razor," and Madame Roland de la Planière shouted from the scaffold: "Oh liberty, what crimes are committed in thy name!" (As for fraternity, Metternich remarked at that time that, if he had a brother, he would prefer to call him cousin.) One can hardly imagine a more tragic fate than that of Chrétien de Malesherbes, a liberal royalist and counsel of the King in court. He was forced to watch as his daughter, his son-in-law, and their children were beheaded before his turn finally came.

It must be remembered that almost everything the Rev-olution had originally aimed for—liberality, humaneness, tolerance, the things that were constantly spoken about—existed under enlightened royal absolutism. Not many years lay between the abolition of capital punishment by Catherine the Great in Russia and Grand Duke Leopold in Tuscany and the invention of the guillotine. A revealing exchange of words took place between Lavoisier's counsel and the judge at his trial:

> Counsel: "You are condemning to death a great scholar!"
> Judge: "The Republic does not need scholars."

Spiritually the French Revolution was a blend of fanat-ically upheld and contradictory positions but, as with most revolutions, it revealed man's true nature. How right Bernanos was when he wrote in his *Les Enfants Humiliés* that humanity is a slimy pulp, and if it were not for the saints and the heroes, the term "man" could not be used. Alexander Hamilton expressed himself even more suc-cinctly when he said to George Washington: "The people,

Sir, your people is a great beast." And the Scriptures, too, declare unmistakably in Genesis 8, 21: "From childhood on, man's mind is turned toward evil."

In the French Revolution the worst sons of France lived out their diabolic drives. Marat, the "people's friend," demanded not only 100,000 death sentences, he also ordered the amputation of noses and ears, the splitting of tongues, the flaming stakes. Charlotte Corday put an end to the life of this devilish democratic fundamentalist. We, in the heart of modern Europe, on the other hand, recently had quite a different type of young lady. Ulrike Meinhof, the famous German leftist terrorist, at her trial, defended Auschwitz, shouting: "Only capitalist money-Jews perished there!" A unique monster? In the preface to his political comedy *On the Rocks*, George Bernard Shaw spoke in favor of genocide—if it were handled humanely and did not arouse lust. The great Shaw, too, a monster? Not at all. Just a parlor pink and, like Archbishop Tutu, a Nobel laureate.

In our age of radical stultification through the mass media, however, and contrary to all warnings, the French Revolution is celebrated. The average man, caught up in his hopeless limitations, clings to his beloved clichés. (I can well imagine that on January 30, 2033, the *Machtübernahme*, the assumption of power by the Nazis, will be commemorated with public festivities.) Robbed of his clichés, he would be forced to think, study, consider, and finally change his picture of history. But such an elitist procedure cannot be asked from the poor wretch.

PORTRAITS AND PROPAGANDA IN THE FRENCH REVOLUTION AND NAPOLEONIC ERA

SAM KNECHT

Sam Knecht is associate professor of art and chairman of the art department at Hillsdale College. An accomplished painter who specializes in both watercolor and egg tempera processes, he holds a master of fine arts degree from the University of Michigan. His paintings have won awards in numerous regional competitions. Articles on his work have appeared in American Artist *and the* Michigan Natural Resources *magazine. In 1985, he was guest professor of drawing for the University of Michigan's program in Florence, Italy, where he taught "Drawing in Florence."*

IN THIS PAPER a survey of paintings and prints which reflect the epoch of the French Revolution will be analyzed. You will be presented with pictures which portray the appearance and lifestyle of people in France before and during the period of revolution at the end of the eighteenth century. Taking a little "liberté," we will continue with images of the Napoleonic era which flowed out of the consequences and conflicts of the Revolution. Made in the years before the French invented photography, these images exist as an interpretive record of the faces of some of the prime movers in the drama of the revolution. Some of the pivotal events likewise have been depicted by the painter's brush or the engraver's burin.

Seeing them makes us believe this chapter of European history truly happened. However, not everything we will see is a factual account. Indeed, some of the most influential artists of the time were geniuses of propaganda and myth-making. In general, Paris was glorified as the art capital of Europe. The Louvre became one of the largest warehouses of great art. Yet equally significant is the fact that during this period artists were not merely front row observers of major political events. At least one, Jacques Louis David, was a main stage player.

Whether performing their customary role as observers or the atypical role of political power brokers, artists were influential because of their effectiveness at communicating with images. "Seeing is believing" was understood then as now. Painters were eighteenth-century counterparts to television cameramen. We should realize that what they depicted often possessed no more truth than today's television docudramas. Still, they could be extraordinarily influential. At the very least they offer a rich sense of the fiery spirit of the times.

A decidedly unfiery, official portrait of King Louis XVI is displayed in **Figure 1.** Smug and serenely self-confident, his expression betrays no inkling of the disasters in store for him. A gracefully-poised right hand steadies his royal sceptre. His head is coiffed nicely with a powdered wig. Both his expansive gesture and the background hint at the enormous power of the French monarchy and the extent of French empire. The painting should not be mistaken as a close likeness, nor does it offer any glimpse into the character of the man. It is pure symbol. Incidentally, note the venerable insignia of the French kings, the gold *fleur-de-lis*, embroidered onto his robe. (Napoleon would later produce a clever substitute for that pattern.)

The King was well-isolated from the subjects whose

affection and allegiance he presumed to enjoy. The sumptuous palace of Versailles (**Fig. 2**) was located a few miles outside of Paris. Begun in the 1670s by Louis XIV, its spectacular furnishings were enjoyed often by Louis XVI before his demise. In October 1789, a desperate and hungry mob including many women marched on the palace. Terrible violence ensued. Royal troops defended Versailles, and the royal family fled to its palace inside Paris.

During earlier and quieter years, Madame Pompadour, portrayed by court painter Boucher (**Fig. 3**), was herself the mistress of King Louis XV. Like a skilled jeweler, Boucher polished every surface of her form into flattering gracefulness. The result is a kind of aloof cameo. She was free to enjoy a life of pleasure as yet another glittering possession of the King.

In her turn, Queen Marie Antoinette (**Fig. 4**) squandered money on frivolous entertainments, ignored the financial crisis the government was suffering, and was callously indifferent to the starvation of peasants.

The painting titled *The Swing* by Fragonard (**Fig. 5**) seems to sum up the frivolity of the privileged classes in France. The setting is the garden of a palace. A pretty young rich girl takes her fun in a swing with a comfortably upholstered seat. Behind her a clergyman does the honors of propelling her forward in a seemingly innocent activity. What the preacher fails to see is the girl's lover, the young gentleman strategically hidden in the bushes at the lower left. In his direction she allows her dainty foot to toss its slipper giving us a rather naughty glimpse of a bare foot. But one guesses that her lover sees even more from his vantage point as he pushes aside a branch to improve his view. Erotic humor was intentional and fashionable in many such artworks collected by the rich at this time. The colors are pastel and delicate. The background trees look like green-tinted puffs of cotton candy—as evanescent as the lifestyle of the aristocrats would prove to be.

But what about the bourgeoisie, at this time? They had their own painters such as Chardin who, in such paintings as *Grace at Table* (**Fig. 6**), suggested that middle class folks were hard-working, humble, and virtuous souls. In contrast to the rococo fashions displayed in Boucher and Fragonard canvasses, Chardin's subjects wear plain, homespun clothing devoid of frills and toned in the browns and greys of cheap dyes. A few well-scrubbed white aprons and caps relieve the dullness of their garb. Their simple piety is emphasized by Chardin. We detect a different kind of myth-making going on here, a sense that the common folk are virtuous in contrast to the amoral aristocrats. One wonders whether they and their families would be among those who would keep their faith or call for the ouster of the Catholic Church from France.

A more strident tone was set by the painter Greuze, who was known for his paintings which teach a moral lesson (**Fig. 7**). His paintings preached to the middle class with a melodramatic sense of social responsibility. This approach found support among officials in the Royal Academy of Art. Ironically enough, the academy was under the sponsorship of the King even though such didactic art contrasts vividly with the delicate rococo fantasies favored by his court.

Among those who were in the business of elevating Reason during the Enlightenment was Voltaire (**Fig. 8**). He was known for his sharp wit in works such as *Candide*. His criticism of established institutions in France led to his imprisonment in the Bastille on more than one occasion and his exile from the country. He, incidentally, was a leading critic of the Catholic Church, which he felt promoted superstition.

Another figure of many talents who would play an important role in the period was Lavoisier (**Fig. 9**). The science-minded reader may remember Lavoisier as the originator of the Law of Conservation of Matter. (That is, matter can neither be created nor destroyed. All mass, however changed in a chemical reaction, still exists and can be accounted for.) Lavoisier wrote the first chemical equation and gave the first sensible explanations of the mysteries of fire. He was typical of the men of science who viewed the universe entirely in rational terms and helped give rise to the label, the Enlightenment. Here, Lavoisier and his elegant wife are shown with some of the apparati he designed for his experiments. He had been awarded a medal from the Royal Academy of Science for his street lighting plan for Paris. Lavoisier was also a member of the company which collected taxes for the government. As such, he was regarded as an aristocrat by the revolutionaries who executed him and fellow company members on the guillotine. This was especially tragic since during his lifetime he had done much to improve farming methods as well as other social conditions in France. While still alive, though, he had had ample opportunity to appreciate the talent of the man who painted his portrait, Jacques Louis David. David was the leading artist of the neoclassical movement, which, among other things, promoted Greco-Roman subject matter, civic virtue, and austere style.

Jacques Louis David's *Oath of the Horatii* (**Fig. 10**) did much to galvanize the will of men of influence. To be sure, it was not viewed by many ordinary people, but it was notorious among the *philosophes*, the liberal thinkers inclined toward a new society based on natural rights. Ironically, the canvas was commissioned by the King and its subject was drawn from a play by the French playwright Corneille based upon an ancient Roman work by Plutarch. The theme of the work is swearing loyalty to the state. It is a kind of Marine's *Semper Fidelis* for its time. Yet what the King did not bargain for was the interpretation by revolutionaries that the painting stood for steadfast adherence to principles of justice and order in a republican, not monarchical state.

Actually, the moment of oath-swearing that David chose is probably his own invention, however much the painting seems like a tableau on a stage set. Such an oath does not occur in Corneille's play. The storyline goes something like this: The Horatii family represents Rome in a bloody war with a traditional enemy. The opposing sides agree to end the struggle with a duel to the death to be fought by a handful of their best fighting men. The three Horatii sons pledge their swords and lives for Rome and will go off to battle brothers from the rival Curatii family. Sisters of the Horatii are shown here swooning and weeping from the conviction that surely at least one of their brothers must die. But what the brothers and their father do not know at this time is that one of the women is secretly betrothed to a rival, Curatius, and that she weeps for his fate.

Skillfully, David made use of contrast in this painting. There is the contrast of latent masculine violence and the limp vulnerability of the feminine principals. Notice the exposed arms and legs of the men whose limbs appear like bundles of steel cables. Helmets and swords gleam in a hard, cold light against the shadows of empty and ominous archways in the background. The sisters huddle together on the right, joined by an anonymous widow with her children, a suggestion that more widows will be created soon.

We find our eyes riveted to the arms and swords of the men. Those arms seem joined to one body just as the swords are joined together in the father's grip. As Sir Kenneth Clark has noted, the sons' arms seem like spokes of a wheel rotating slowly within the frozen silence of the painting. Clearly evident is the resolve of the father who pledges his sons' lives to the state. He looks not at his offspring but rather at their weapons, the tools of their service. The swords stand for the cutting loose of the old order of selfishness, sentimentality, and family attachments as typified by the women at the right.

As writer Michel Le Bris has observed:

> Each one reveals himself, recreated, "liberated" from himself in a new alliance. The Horatii, at the moment of battle, renounce themselves so as to belong only to their oath. The acceptance of death marks both the birth of the community and their own birth ... these are really new men who will cleave like swords.

Despite what one ordinarily senses in a gesture of extending an open hand, David used the gesture of the open palm to represent exposing oneself openly to the probability of death in a righteous struggle. This is the kind of picture that demands self-sacrifice, even martyrdom.

David spent many months in Rome working on this painting and researching its historical details meticulously. The French people were already finding their interests in ancient Rome stirred by recent French-run excavations at Pompeii. David's painting gained added weight with its legacy of the grandeur and justice of the republican Roman order. With revolutionary sentiment stirred by paintings such as this, the divine right of kings was presented with one of its most serious challenges.

David followed up the impact of his Horatii in the fateful year of 1789 with this work, *Lictors Bearing the Bodies of the Dead Sons of Brutus* (**Fig. 11**), which shows the result of treason against the state. Brutus had been made aware that his sons were plotting a coup against him to bring a war to a halt and placate his enemies. He ordered their arrest and execution. The women of the family dissolve into hysterical grief as the corpses of the sons are carried past. Once more, duty to the state transcends family bonds.

David soon left the life of artistic meditation to join the active field of politics. He was a member of the Estates-

General and swore the Oath of the Tennis Court calling for the drafting of a constitution. He made a sketch of the event shown in **Figure 12.**

Despite the fact that King Louis allowed the existence of the new National Assembly, he began to marshall his army to break it up. Meanwhile, the masses in Paris took action. On July 14, 1789, a huge crowd rushed to the Bastille prison and took it over, hoping to find weapons and ammunition with which to defend themselves from the King's troops (**Fig. 13**). Immediately a revolutionary government was declared in Paris by a number of leaders.

Eventually the King plotted with friends in Austria and Prussia to wage war against the revolutionary government in hopes of regaining his power. Finally, in August of 1792, the King and his family were arrested and imprisoned. David (**Fig. 14**) had been given the Directorship of the Committee on Public Education, a very important post in the Legislative Assembly. As such, he was friends with the radical Robespierre. He designed a ceremony at Robespierre's request which dedicated a statue of Reason as the ranking deity in France, thus banishing the superstitious beliefs of Catholicism. With Robespierre, David voted for the death of the King.

Thus, on January 21, 1793, King Louis XVI was guillotined, as depicted in a contemporary print (**Fig. 15**). The National Convention was formed to write a new constitution abolishing the monarchy and establishing new rights and laws. The radical Jacobin element of which David was a part did not have complete control over the new Convention. They were opposed by the Girondists, a more moderate faction. When the Jacobins led by Robespierre and Jean Paul Marat expelled the Girondists from the Convention, the Girondists retaliated.

In July, the Girondist Charlotte Corday assassinated Jean Paul Marat in his bath (**Fig. 16**). David, called upon by his fellows in the Convention, immediately went to work memorializing the martyr. Sir Kenneth Clark called this work "the greatest political picture ever painted. . . . The figure, no less than the wooden box and the *trompe l'oeil* papers, gives the impression of absolute truth, even though we know that Marat's face and body were ravaged by disease which David dared not represent."

The bathtub which Marat used so often to ease the pain of excema sores now serves as his chill coffin. The upper half of the canvas is filled with a shadowy blankness, an eloquent space which dramatically sets off the spotlit face and arms of Marat. Marat has the expression of a fulfilled martyr. A sophisticated art lover would have noticed David's use of Michelangelo's *Pieta* as the basis for Marat's pose. The symbolism is unmistakable. Note the proximity of Charlotte Corday's knife and the quill pen still grasped by Marat. The prominence of the pen and its products suggest that Marat's words and ideas will overcome the deed of assassination.

Later that same year, hundreds of people suspected of being either sympathetic to the King or against the reforming policies of the revolutionary government had been rounded up and imprisoned. By September, vigilante groups had broken into the prisons and killed over a thousand prisoners. The Reign of Terror ensued with more than 17,000 death sentences handed out by the Convention. In October, Marie Antoinette was dressed ignominiously in a plain dress and cap and led off to meet the guillotine. That final day in her life was recorded in a sketch made by David (**Fig. 17**).

Robespierre's enemies in the Convention took the upper hand, arrested him, and had him executed in 1794. David was thrown in prison and feared his own execution, but he was eventually released. By 1795, things had not completely quieted down, as the painting by Delacroix seen in **Figure 18** indicates. Here a mob rushes into the Convention chamber with the head of a guillotine victim waving about on a long pike.

The impact of so much bloodshed even made its way into fashion. During the Reign of Terror it became fashionable for women to wear gowns with red bands crossed over the chest or back to symbolize that one had a relative imprisoned or victimized by the guillotine. More graphic still was the style adopted by a few of wearing a thin red ribbon around the neck. **Figure 19** displays dresses fashioned in the revolutionary style. Simple bonnets were adopted to eschew aristocratic elegance. High-waisted dresses show the influence of ancient republican Roman fashions as inspired by paintings unearthed at Pompeii.

After he had been made a general in the army, Napoleon posed for some sketches made by David (**Fig. 20**). David was in a good position to observe the Corsican's meteoric rise in military rank and his political takeover as First Consul in 1799. In Napoleon, David, like other revolutionaries, saw a man of decisive action and proven leadership skills. Surely this seemed a man who could help realize the aims of the Revolution which had gotten bogged down by political in-fighting as well as external wars.

David made another study of the general (**Fig. 21**) in which it is interesting to note the romantic tendencies: Napoleon wears long, sweptback hair. The reader will note that long-haired cultural heroes did not make their first appearance in the rock-and-roll decade of the 1960s. Soon enough, however, Napoleon had his hair cropped more closely, probably in emulation of the style of ancient Roman emperors who were his inspiration (**Fig. 22**).

David became one of Napoleon's darlings, since he did much to extoll the heroic exploits of Napoleon and his troops. The artist commemorated the famous crossing of the Alps (**Fig. 23**). In this canvas a resolute general points the way for his men. Surely this helped fuel the notion that Napoleon was the man of destiny for all of France—a man of destiny whose deeds strike a classical chord with the reference to Hannibal.

More mythmaking goes on in **Figure 24** with Napoleon

taking time out from his victory at Jaffa in the Near East to visit a pest house, a building filled with plague-stricken prisoners he is liberating. They seem to be rising almost from death like Lazarus. An effective piece of propaganda, the picture suggests Napoleon has the miraculous powers of a savior who can heal with his touch.

The theme of martyrdom also continued to fascinate French artists such as Girodet who glorified the soldiers who fought in Napoleon's wars (**Fig. 25**). The scene, incidentally, is not heaven, but Valhalla, as popularized in faked romantic epics about Ossian, a brave and ancient Celtic warrior.

Not only were myths venerating Napoleon's exploits generated on canvas. There were architectural opportunities in Paris to express the spirit that a new age had dawned. With its neoclassical exterior, the church of La Madeleine simulated ancient Roman temples (**Fig. 26**). Thus it served as a monumental symbol that the Napoleonic empire was a modern update of the Roman empire. Such was the movement to purify the Parisian cityscape without reference to the French Gothic style of the medieval and Baroque style of the monarchical past.

Another step supplanting traditional French architecture is a sidelight of *Le Sacre* (The Coronation) by David (**Fig. 27**). The coronation took place in the cathedral of Notre Dame whose interior was temporarily outfitted with stage flats so that it would resemble the interior of a Roman temple rather than a Catholic church. Feeling, however, that he must defer somewhat to tradition and the continuing position of the Catholic Church in France, Napoleon decided to have a coronation ceremony with no less than Pope Pius VII dragged in from Rome. The Pope, with his concern for temporal as well as spiritual matters, was strongly opposed to Napoleon. Practically on the eve of the coronation he refused to be involved because Napoleon had wed Josephine earlier in a mere civil cere-

Fig. 1, A.F. Callet, *Portrait of Louis XVI*, 18th c.

Fig. 2, Versailles

Fig. 3, François Boucher, *Madame de Pompadour*, 1759

Fig. 4, Elisabeth-Louise Vigée-Lebrun, *Marie Antoinette and Her Children*, 1778

Fig. 6, Jean-Baptiste-Siméon Chardin, *Grace at Table*, 1740

Fig. 5, Jean-Honoré Fragonard, *The Swing*, 1766

Fig. 7, Jean-Baptiste Greuze, *The Return of the Prodigal Son*, 1777–78

Fig. 8, Jean Antoine Houdon, *Voltaire*, 1781

Fig. 9, Jacques Louis David, *Portrait of M. and Mme. Lavoisier,* 1788

Fig. 10, Jacques Louis David, *Oath of the Horatii,* 1784

Fig. 11, Jacques Louis David, *Lictors Bringing Brutus the Bodies of His Sons,* 1789

Fig. 12, Jacques Louis David, *The Oath of the Tennis Court*, 1789

Fig. 13, Anonymous, *Storming the Bastille*, 18th c.

Fig. 14, Jacques Louis David, *Self-Portrait*, c. 1794

Fig. 15, Anonymous, *Execution of Louis XVI*, 18th c.

Fig. 16, Jacques Louis David, *Death of Marat,* 1793

Fig. 17, Jacques Louis David, *Marie Antoinette on Her Way to the Guillotine,* 1793

Fig. 18, Eugène Delacroix, *Boissy d'Anglas* (*The People Invading the National Convention and Presenting the Head of Jean Feraud on a Pike to Boissy d'Anglas in the Riots of 20 May 1795*), 1831

Fig. 19, Le Sueur Brothers, *Women and Girls*, n.d.

Fig. 20, Jacques Louis David, *Bonaparte,* sketches, 1797

Fig. 21, Jacques Louis David, *Portrait of Napoleon,* unfinished, 1797–98

Fig. 22, Jean-Antoine Gros, *Bonaparte as Consul*, n.d.

Fig. 23, Jacques Louis David, *Napoleon Crossing the Alps*, 1801

Fig. 24, Jean-Antoine Gros, *Pest House at Jaffa*, 1804

Fig. 25, Anne Louis Girodet, *Ossian Receiving the Napoleonic Officers,* 1802

Fig. 26, Church of La Madeleine, Paris, begun 1808

Fig. 27, Jacques Louis David, *Coronation of Napoleon*, 1805

Fig. 28, Jacques Louis David, *Sketches of the Coronation,* c. 1805

Fig. 29, Jacques Louis David, *Napoleon in His Study,* 1812

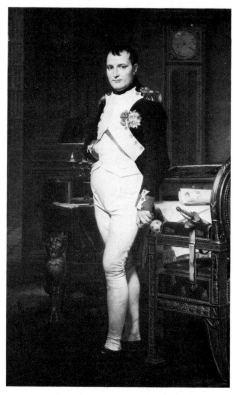

Fig. 30, Antonio Canova, *Napoleon as Mars,* 1803–06

Fig. 31, Jean-Antoine Gros, *Napoleon at Eylau*, 1808

Fig. 32, Francisco Goya, *The Third of May*, 1808

Fig. 33, Francisco Goya, *What More Can Be Done?*, 1810–14

Fig. 34, Théodore Géricault, *Raft of the Medusa*, 1818–19

Fig. 35, Eugène Delacroix, *Liberty Guiding the People*, 1830

mony. A church wedding was hastily arranged to clear away the Pope's resistance.

David's sketch of the event (**Fig. 28**) shows Napoleon placing the crown on his own head, a supremely arrogant gesture. For the finished painting, David opted for Napoleon transferring the crown to Josephine's head, suggesting that since he now assumed absolute power he could confer power upon anyone he favored (**Fig. 27**). Observe the replacement of the *fleur-de-lis* pattern on their robes with the shapes of honeybees, a motif supposedly invented by Napoleon himself. Here we have a suggestion of the collective state symbolized by all the dedicated worker bees who make it up. Notice the figure of the Pope on the far right side of the canvas. Originally when the painting was finished, David simply had the Pope with his hands resting on his lap. Napoleon ordered David to change that pose, saying they had not brought the Pope all the way from Rome to sit there and do nothing. So David obliged and repainted the hand of the Pope so that it was raised slightly in a gesture which could be taken for a benediction. This was not to be the last tension between Pius VII and Napoleon. Eventually, Pius VII excommunicated the French emperor. Napoleon tried to suppress news of that embarrassment and had the Pope imprisoned back in Italy. This must certainly have disturbed those French citizens who still clung to the Catholic faith.

David went on to make another portrait of Napoleon as emperor (**Fig. 29**). With neither the services of a battlefield nor of monumental architecture, David manages to use space and scale in such a way as to lend grandeur to his leader. He opted for a very low eye-level, about the level of Napoleon's desktop. The notoriously short emperor appears quite tall as a result. Upon that desk a candle flickers, almost burned out. This is a clever suggestion that Napoleon has been working well into the night. The clock on the wall reads around four (in the morning, we are led to believe).

Another artist who inflated the Emperor's stature, this time in ludicrous fashion, was the Italian import, Antonio Canova. The statue he carved from fine Carrara marble was superhuman in size; over eleven and a half feet tall (**Fig. 30**). At first Napoleon objected to its nudity. However, Canova, whose reputation as a sculptor was second to none at the time, convinced the emperor that such was the heroic essence of classical art. The classical style in which Canova was a master was necessary to set Napoleon onto an Olympian plane, it was reasoned. (Imagine George Washington looking like this.)

Consider more glorification of Napoleon on the battlefield in the panoramic canvas by Baron Gros (**Fig. 31**). It depicts a lull in the Polish campaign after particularly bloody fighting. Napoleon rides out to survey the human cost. Grisly corpses are heaped up in the foreground. Gros' realistic style depicts a bit of snow which has filtered down on the bodies without really obscuring the ghastly forms. Napoleon rolls his eyes heavenward as if to say, "If only this did not have to happen." Gros intended to suggest that Napoleon was obeying a divine mandate. More accurately, we recognize that Napoleon followed, indeed manufactured, his own flawed mission.

Napoleon hoped to ride the dream of democracy into all the countries of Europe. One of his most vivid failures occurred in Spain. Napoleon invaded Spain and overthrew its tottering monarchy. At first he was welcomed by liberal-thinking Spaniards. Then it became apparent that one form of oppression had been exchanged for another when Napoleon installed his brother, Joseph, as king of Spain. Spanish patriots began fighting a guerrilla war against the French forces of occupation.

Francisco Goya dealt with one of the calamities of the resistance in *The Executions of the Third of May, 1808* (**Fig. 32**). It depicts a French reprisal conducted the day after the poorly armed Spanish had attacked occupation soldiers in the streets of Madrid. In revenge for the casualties his forces suffered, the French commander ordered the execution of hundreds of innocent people rounded up on the streets. Here we see a few victims representative of many more. In their tattered garments they appear helpless, some doomed, others defiant against the aim of the firing squad. One notices on the right the black-capped troops of Napoleon's occupation force blending as a kind of fighting machine. Their bodies and rifles are as bound together in shape and purpose as the men in the *Oath of the Horatii*. Yet in Goya's canvas we understand their intent is evil and not motivated by divine will. The ideals of the French Revolution had been betrayed. The sublimation of self in service to the state has become so extended as to sanction all kinds of atrocity.

Goya's eyes did not blink, nor did his engraving tools waver when he recorded more of what the French did in Spain. The ghastly scene in **Figure 33** is but one of many Goya depicted in his series on the disasters of war.

Eventually Napoleon met his demise. With his defeat and ultimate departure from the European stage France was to suffer more years of political turmoil. During the decades following the failure of the Revolution and Napoleonic era, artists grew pessimistic in outlook. They mistrusted the institutions of church and state, and the old order of any kind. The earlier generation of artists such as David and Gros gave way to a new generation of romantics such as Gericault and Delacroix. The former had put much stock in reason and controlled technique. The latter asserted that feeling and impulsive expressions were paramount.

One canvas which sums up the gloomy worldview of the post-Napoleonic era is the *Raft of the Medusa* by Gericault (**Fig. 34**). In particular it was understood as a direct criticism of the Bourbon government of the reinstated monarch. Shipping masters who enjoyed political favors and protection had allowed a number of maritime disasters to take place. In this case, a frigate, *The Medusa*, overloaded with passengers, foundered in waters off the coast. The captain ordered many of the passengers to be put overboard on makeshift rafts and set adrift to lighten the load of the boat. Gericault depicts a disordered heap of castaways, some already dead, the rest suffering from days without food and water. Their bodies are intertwined in serpentine fashion, a composition in ominous accord with the name of the ship. Despite the sighting of a distant ship and a brief flurry of hope, a mood of despair seems to dominate. In universal terms Gericault suggests that the whole world consists of people who are adrift, tossed hither and yon by forces over which they have no control. This is the repudiation of a belief that the world is governed by reason or Divine Providence. It insists upon reminding us of the human capacity for evil and degradation.

Succeeding waves of discontent led to the Revolution of 1830, which was immortalized in the painting, *Liberty Guiding the People*, by Delacroix (**Fig. 35**). The general public mistakenly assumes that this canvas was inspired by the first French Revolution of 1789. Despite its brilliance of conception and style it must be understood as a work of pure mythmaking and propaganda. It is as much a call to arms as *The Oath of the Horatii*. Delacroix was as deeply concerned with moving the hearts and minds of the French as had been David and Gros. Like them, he employed artistic symbols to embody a set of political purposes. Here Liberty is personified as a bare-breasted Venus type, another borrowing from the Greco-Roman past. She injects herself into the street fighting in Paris in 1830 and into the midst of the proletariat, bourgeoisie, and student archetypes who lead the current revolution. One imagines that any red-blooded Frenchman would follow her to the gates of Hell itself. The French tricolor is at the apex of the composition and its colors are repeated throughout the rest of the painting. Once again men sacrifice their lives to the spirit of revolution leaving historians to debate what was gained.

In conclusion, the artists surveyed in this paper portrayed the ideas, individuals, and events of the Revolution of 1789 and its aftermath in a revealing manner. Each used visual images to express a political viewpoint. One of the chief ingredients in all these works has been propaganda, whether present in large or small amounts. Distortion, exaggeration, shock tactics, and the myths of Greece and Rome were the most common devices used to convey the artists' political sense. One should not confuse these images with objective fact. Nevertheless, they stand as some of the essential records of the spirit of the times. The epoch demanded political commitment. Some artists such as David were well-situated to influence the thinking of both revolutionaries and common people. The aim of each artist, whether misguided or wise, no matter what his style, was to state passionately his desire for a better order of things in Europe.

THE ARMED DOCTRINE
IN FICTION

RUSSELL KIRK

*For more than three decades, Russell Kirk has been in the
thick of the intellectual controversies of our time. His book*
The Conservative Mind: From Burke to Santayana, *reprinted
often since its original publication (Regnery, 1953), is widely
regarded as the seminal work of the modern conservative
movement. Author of a syndicated column for many years, as
well as 28 books, and more than 500 articles, essays, and
short stories, he is also the editor of the* University Bookman
and founder of Modern Age. *In one of his final presidential
acts, Ronald Reagan publicly presented Dr. Kirk with the
Presidential Citizen's Medal.*

WE ARE MOVED far more by images than by logic-
chopping. What Americans think of the Russian Revolution has been much influenced, in recent decades, by the
films *Dr. Zhivago* and *Nicholas and Alexandra*—
productions, happily, which are both truthful and imaginative. The recent French film *Danton* fixes in our minds
a sound impression of how revolutions devour their children. Most "soap opera" productions on television nowadays, on the other hand, inflict upon the American public
images that are trivial, banal, or corrupting—damage,
especially to the young, not easily undone.

I am concerned here, however, not with the theater,
films, or television, but with the older and more long-

lasting form of imagery called the novel—which attained the height of its influence during the nineteenth century, but still makes a powerful impression, frequently, on the imagination and the general assumptions of such men and women as remain culturally literate. What important works of fiction have formed the public's understanding of the French Revolution? Before I commence to answer that question, however, permit me to define my terms. By "the armed doctrine" in the title of this essay, I mean ideology—that is, a system of political dogmata, fanatically held. Edmund Burke called Jacobinism, the triumphant ideology of the French Revolution, "an armed doctrine"; Britain was then combating, Burke said, not merely the power of France, but a fanatic political creed, a kind of inverted religion, preached originally at Paris in a secularized Dominican monastery but within a few years disseminated throughout Europe and even in Britain.

Since then, there have been inflicted upon our civilization such ideologies as communism, anarchism, syndicalism, and Naziism, together with Asiatic and African variations on these themes. The armed doctrine I propose to discuss today is Jacobinism, or the French levelling frenzy, and the fashion in which it was perceived and represented to the public by three important novelists.

Sainte-Beuve, somewhere in his *Causeries du Lundi*, tells us of a Parisian playwright watching from his window a ferocious mob pouring through the street below. "See my pageant passing!" the dramatist exclaims. The imaginary happenings represented on the stage have worked upon the imagination of a mercurial public already excited by social disruption; and so the pageant has taken on flesh in the streets, perhaps for harm.

The French Revolution itself, in no small part, was produced by the idyllic imagination of Rousseau and other visionaries of the Enlightenment. It would be possible to show how the fiction of Rousseau, Voltaire, and other French men of letters had revolutionary consequences in fairly short order. Here, however, I am limiting the discussion to *reflections* of the French Revolution—and more particularly of that armed doctrine Jacobinism—in English and French literature after the event. It would be interesting to discuss the revolutionary spirit that animated the poet Shelley and Mary Shelley; or the reaction against the French Revolution as expressed in poetry by Coleridge and Wordsworth. But having little time, I restrict myself to the novel.

I commence with a *jeu d'esprit* of Jean Francois de La Harpe, satirist, playwright, critic, and friend of Voltaire. A supporter of the Mountain and other extreme revolutionaries during the terrible years of 1792 and 1793, nevertheless La Harpe was flung into prison in 1794. In this peril he turned ardent Catholic and champion of the old order. Among his papers, when he died in 1803, was discovered what Sainte-Beuve calls La Harpe's best work, *The Prophecy of Cazotte.* This is fiction, and yet very true. In it, La Harpe uses as his mouthpiece Jacques Cazotte, a mystical author of romances and one of the brotherhood of the illuminati. A very real person, Cazotte declared that he possessed the gift of prophecy; he was guillotined in September 1792. Here I give you this fictitious prophecy of Cazotte, in H. A. Taine's precis of La Harpe's fable.

> It seems to me [La Harpe writes] as if it were but yesterday, and yet it is at the beginning of the year 1788. We were dining with one of our confreres of the Academy, a grand seignoir and a man of intelligence. The company was numerous and of every profession, courtiers, advocates, men of letters and academicians; all had feasted luxuriously according to custom. At the dessert, the wines of Malvoisie and of Constance contributed to the gayety [sic] a sort of freedom not always kept with decorous limits. At that time society had reached the point at which

everything may be expressed that excites laughter. Champfort had read to us his impious and libertine stories, and great ladies had listened to these without recourse to their fans. Hence a deluge of witticisms against religion, one quoting a tirade from "La Pucelle," another bringing forward certain philo- sophical stanzas by Diderot . . . and with unbounded applause. . . . The conversation becomes more se- rious; admiration is expressed at the revolution ac- complished by Voltaire and all agree in its being the first title to his fame. "He gave the tone to his cen- tury, finding readers in the antechambers as well as in the drawing-room." One of the guests narrates, bursting with laughter, what a hairdresser said to him while powdering his hair: "You see, sir, although I am a miserable scrub, I have no more religion than anyone else." They conclude that the Revolution will soon be consummated, that superstition and fanati- cism must wholly give way to philosophy, and they thus calculate the probabilities of the epoch and those of the future society which will see the reign of reason. The most aged lament not being able to flatter themselves that they will see it; the young people rejoice in a reasonable prospect of seeing it, and espe- cially do they congratulate the Academy on having paved the way for the great work and in having been the headquarters, the centre, the inspirer of freedom of thought.

One of the guests had taken no part in this gay conversation . . . a person named Cazotte, an amiable and original man, but, unfortunately, infatuated with the reveries of the illuminati. In the most serious tones he begins: —"Gentlemen," says he, "be con- tent; you will witness this great revolution that you so much desire. You know that I am something of a prophet, and I repeat it, you will witness it. . . . Do you know the result of this revolution, for all of you, so soon as you remain here?"—"Ah!" exclaims Condorcet, with his shrewd, simple air and smile, "let us see, a philosopher is not sorry to encounter a prophet."—"You, Monsieur de Condorcet, will expire stretched on the floor of a dungeon; you will die of the poison you take to escape the executioner, of the poison which the felicity of that era will compel you always to carry about your person!" At first, great astonishment was manifested and then came an outburst of laughter. "What has all this in common with philosophy and the reign of reason?"—"Precisely what I have just remarked to you: in the name of philosophy, of humanity, of freedom, under the reign of reason, you will thus reach your end; and, evidently, the reign of reason will arrive, for there will be temples of reason, and, in those days, in all France, the temples will be those alone of reason.... You, Monsieur de Champfort, you will sever your veins with twenty-two strokes of a razor and yet you will not die for months afterwards. You, Monsieur Vicq-d'Azir, you will not open your own veins, but you will have them opened six times in one day, in the agonies of gout, so as to be more certain of success, and you will die that night. You, Monsieur de Nicolai, on the scaffold, you, Monsieur Bailly, on the scaffold; you, Monsieur de Malesherbes, on the scaffold ... you, Monsieur Rocher, also on the scaffold."—"But then we shall have been overcome by Turks or Tartars?"—"By no means; you will be governed as I have already told you, solely by philosophy and reason. Those who are to treat you in this manner will all be philosophers, will all, at every moment, have on their lips the phrases you have uttered within the hour, will repeat your maxims, will quote, like yourselves, the stanzas of Diderot and of 'La Pucelle' "—"And when will all this happen?"—"Six years will not pass before what I tell you will be accomplished."—"Well, these are miracles," exclaims La Harpe, "and you leave me out?"—"You will be no less a miracle, for you will then be a Christian."—"Ah," interposes Champfort, "I breathe again; if we are to die only when La Harpe becomes a Christian, we are immortals."—"As for that, we women," says the Duchesse of Gramont "are extremely fortunate in being of no consequence in revolutions. It is understood that we are not to blame, and our sex. . . ."—"Your sex, ladies, will not protect you this time. . . . You will be treated precisely as men, with no difference whatever. . . . You, Madame la Duchesse, will be led to the scaffold, you and many ladies besides yourself, in a cart with your hands tied behind your back."—"Ah, in that event, I hope to have at least a carriage covered with black."—"No, Madame, greater ladies than yourself will go, like yourself, in a cart and with their hands tied like yours." "Greater ladies! What, princesses of the blood!"—"Still greater ladies than those. . . ." They begin to think the jest carried too far. Madame de Gramont, to dispel the gloom, did not insist upon a reply to her last exclamation, contenting herself by saying in the lightest tone, "And they will not leave one even a confessor."—"No, madame, neither you nor any other person will be allowed a confessor; the last of the condemned that will have one, as act of grace, will be. . . ." He stopped a moment. "Tell me, now, who is the fortunate mortal enjoying this pre-rogative?"—"It is the last that will remain to him, and it will be the King of France."

All this came to pass, as you know; and Cazotte himself, in 1792, despite his daughter's noble efforts to save him, had his head taken off by the guillotine. Truly truth is stranger than fiction.

The penitence of such sometime revolutionaries as La Harpe was not lost upon English men of letters. Let us turn to one of the most widely read of these, Charles Dickens.

When I was a schoolboy, *A Tale of Two Cities* was studied in most American high schools: more than anything else, it formed young people's minds concerning the French Revolution. Charles Dickens' mind on that subject had been formed by Thomas Carlyle's famous book, published twenty-two years earlier. In 1859, when *A Tale of Two Cities* was published, Dickens was a Radical—but in the English signification of that political term. He was deeply concerned, as was Carlyle, for the condition of the poor; and, again like Carlyle, he aspired to clear away old abuses and archaic clutter in the civil social order. But Jacobin radicalism, fiercely ideological, repelled him—to put it mildly: it was inhumane, sacrificing men and women to political abstractions. Englishmen in general do not take to ideology, being empirical in their politics; and nobody was more English than Charles Dickens.

A Tale of Two Cities begins with much description, as of 1775, of the wretchedness, and near-starvation, of the French lower classes, both urban and rural. We are introduced to an evil Marquis, apparently intended by Dickens to represent the nobility of France; this unpleasant character is as unreal as Sir John Chester, in Dickens' other historical novel, *Barnaby Rudge*; Dickens did not move in English country-house society, let alone the titled families of France. (When he and his friend Wilkie Collins made expeditions to Paris, it was not to spy out the nakedness of the land, but rather that of its women.) As A. W. Ward remarks in his biography of the great novelist, "If Dickens desired to depict the noble of the *ancien régime*, either according to Carlyle or to intrinsic probability, he should not have offered, in his Marquis, a type historically questionable, and unnatural besides."

In short, Dickens sternly reproaches the Old Regime

across the Channel—even somewhat unjustly, perhaps; the lack of wheaten bread, after all, was the result not of public policy or private selfishness, but of crop failure— what is termed an act of God. With Carlyle, he looks upon the outbreak of the Revolution as a judgment; in Carlyle's words:

> When the age of Miracles lay faded into the distance as an incredible tradition, and even the age of Conventionalities was now old; and Man's Existence had for long generations rested on mere formulas which were grown hollow by course of time, and it seemed as if no Reality any longer existed, but only Phantasms of realities, and God's Universe were the work of the Tailor and the Upholsterer mainly, and men were buckram masks that went about becking and grimacing there,—on a sudden, the Earth yawns asunder, and amid Tartarean smoke, and glare of fierce brightness, rises Sansculottism, many-headed, fire-breathing, and asks, "What think ye of me?"

Once Sansculotte has burst forth, however, Dickens will not embrace him fraternally—no, indeed. Defarge of the wine-shop, cannonier at the storming of the Bastille, is hating and hateful, though retaining some affection for his old master Doctor Manette; Madame Defarge, of the knitting needles, is quite merciless; and the portrait of Jacques Third, Defarge's henchman, is that of a monstrous sadist, "with his cruel fingers at his hungry mouth." The scenes of the terrorists frantically sharpening their weapons in the courtyard by the bank, and of the blood-stained crew dancing the Carmagnole through the streets, stick in the memory of every reader of the novel. Jerry, the bank porter, whose nocturnal trade is that of grave-robber, is horrified by these slaughtering ideologues: their example converts him to better ways, rather as prison and the sight of the guillotine converted La Harpe to Christianity and royalism.

Dickens finds no revolutionary worthy of the least praise in this tragic novel; his hero is a debauched lawyer, Sidney Carton, who musingly repeats to himself as he walks the Paris streets, "I am the resurrection and the life, saith the Lord: he that believeth in me, though he were dead, yet shall he live: and whosoever liveth and believeth in me, shall never die." And when Carton lays down his life for his friend—or for his friend's wife—there come the lines that still can draw tears from my eyes, "It is a far, far better thing that I do, than I have ever done; it is a far, far better rest that I go to, than I have ever known." And then the blade of the guillotine falls.

It is difficult for anyone who has read *A Tale of Two Cities* to think of the French Revolution as a deliverance from servitude. The zealots for the Armed Doctrine are devilish. "Ha!" said Miss Pross, "it doesn't need an interpreter to explain the meaning of these creatures. They have but one, and it's Midnight, Murder, and Mischief." Miss Pross is a comical Britannica, and here she speaks for what the English people decided about the Armed Doctrine. "For gracious sake, don't talk about Liberty," she continues; "we have quite enough of that."

Thus Charles Dickens, the English Radical, expresses in fiction what Edmund Burke compressed into a sentence: "Men of intemperate mind never can be free; their passions forge their fetters."

The novel about the French Revolution most widely read, during the past century and more, after *A Tale of Two Cities*, is *Ninety-Three*, Victor Hugo's last volume of fiction, published in 1874. Yet Ayn Rand instructs us, in a strange recent edition of this novel, that "*Ninety-Three* is *not* a novel about the French Revolution. . . . The theme of *Ninety-Three*—which is played in brilliantly unexpected variations in all the key incidents of the story, and which is the motive power of all the characters and events, integrating them into an inevitable progression toward a magnificent climax—is *man's loyalty to values.*"

In this, Ayn Rand—who first read Hugo at the age of fourteen, in "the stifling, sordid ugliness of Soviet Russia"—is in sharp disagreement with G. K. Chesterton, in *A Handful of Authors* (a book that presumably she never read, if indeed she ever read anything by Chesterton). There Chesterton, in his essay on Victor Hugo, declares that *Ninety-Three* is "the great novel of the Revolution." He finds in that book a principle scarcely consonant with the dogmata of Ayn Rand: Hugo showed, Chesterton maintains, "that such a sacrifice of individuals became necessary, and in a strange, bitter manner, attractive, even in the modern age."

Here Chesterton refers to Hugo's description in his earlier novels of how the individual was sacrificed to the medieval order (in *Notre Dame de Paris*) and how the individual was sacrificed to "our own modern order of law and judgment and criminal procedure" (in *Les Misérables*). Yet Chesterton, strangely enough, seems to approve, very nearly, Hugo's sacrifice of the individual to an ideology of democracy; indeed, Chesterton shows at least a sneaking fondness for "The great demagogues of the Terror . . . so filled with the unifying convictions, that their life became a poetical unity, a work of art like the legend of a medieval saint."

Now Hugo, by 1874, approved of the demagogues of the Terror of 1793. Early in life, Hugo had been a Catholic and a royalist, so reared by his mother; under his soldier-father's influence, he became first a Revolutionary partisan and then a Bonapartist; in his middle years, he had thought the Terror a blot upon the Revolution. But by the time he wrote *Ninety-Three*, he had come to think that the Terror had been necessary, and even praiseworthy, as a means of breaking the old order and ushering in the new. The course of French politics during Hugo's lifetime, and since his death in 1885, scarcely has justified Hugo's notion that breaking with the past must bring on a future of general happiness.

107

Ninety-Three is a novel of ideology. It is set in the forests of Brittany, where the peasants held out to the last for church and king, against the columns of soldiery dispatched from Paris by the Jacobins. On the one side is the Jacobin ideology, in the person of Gauvain, an idealistic young nobleman who has embraced the Revolutionary cause; also in the much grimmer person of Cimourdain, a former priest who has discarded religious faith for ideological fanaticism—a type not unfamiliar in the year 1989. On the other side is a kind of Legitimist ideology, represented by the fearless and merciless Marquis de Lantenac, eighty years old, a fanatic champion and would-be restorer of the Old Regime; indeed, of feudalism.

The Marquis is the head of a great Breton house; Gauvain, his opponent in the field, is the Marquis' nephew. And Cimourdain, *ci-devant* priest, what we would call now a political commissar, dispatched by Marat, Danton, and Robespierre to keep a jealous eye on the young military genius Gauvain—why, Cimourdain, the complete ideologue, has been Gauvain's tutor in past years; and although Cimourdain in theory loves all humankind, the only real human being he loves is Gauvain.

With the exception of Gauvain, Hugo's Jacobins are repellent. At the beginning of the second book of *Ninety-Three*, Hugo makes us privy to a meeting of Robespierre, Danton, and Marat: he pins to them the names of Greek monsters—Minos, Aecacus, and Rhadamanthus. And indeed they are repellent, physically and morally. Robespierre is pale and cold, with "a nervous twitching in his cheek, which must have hindered him from smiling." Danton is disordered in appearance, buttonless: "His face was pitted with smallpox, he had an angry frown between his eyelids, a kindly pucker in the corners of his mouth, thick lips, large teeth, a porter's hand, flashing eyes." As for Marat, "The small man was yellow, and looked deformed when he was seated; he carried his head thrown back, his eyes were bloodshot, there were livid spots on his face; he wore a handkerchief tied over his smooth, greasy hair; he had no forehead, and a terrible, enormous mouth." Their talk is of exterminating enemies, internal and external; and in particular, of destroying the peasants of the Vendée and their aristocrat leaders.

Can Hugo approve of these eminent Jacobins, who have supped so long on horrors? Perhaps—in the sense that they are instruments of revolutionary change, marching toward a secular Zion for all mankind. Can Hugo approve of Cimourdain, who guillotines the one human being he loves, Gauvain? Yes, Hugo can: for the ideologue Cimourdain is what Ayn Rand calls "loyal to values"; he can even approve of Lantenac, for the Breton prince also is "loyal to values"—quite different values, of course. Yet Hugo's heart goes out to the merciful Gauvain, who lets his captive uncle the Marquis go free, and is himself guillotined for that act. Gauvain has betrayed Jacobin "values" in this clash of loyalties; but he has been true to humane impulses. For Hugo, we must conclude, there lies beyond ideology a supreme value of Humanitarianism—also an ideology, though possibly not an Armed Doctrine. As for Cimourdain, after having guillotined Gauvain, he shoots himself: he has been true to his ideological values, but false to human nature.

It is interesting that Hugo's two heroes, the Marquis and Gauvain, are noblemen, even though the younger of them believes in an abstract democracy. When the Marquis de Lantenac successfully makes his retreat from the shattered and burning Tower la Tourge, he halts on hearing the shrieks of a mother and on seeing the peril of three little children trapped in the burning chateau. Then he turns back to rescue the children, though that act will lead to his capture, his execution, and the ruin of his cause in Brittany. Hugo treats this heroic decision as if it were an inexplicable descent of grace upon the Marquis—even though Hugo had rejected the Christian doctrine of grace. "The Marquis de Lantenac has been transfigured," Hugo writes.

Similarly, when Gauvain, overwhelmed by the Marquis' generosity, and remembering the ties of ancient family, sets his uncle free in defiance of ideology—why, Hugo can only write, "The swordbearer had been metamorphosed into an angel of light." Gauvain's tormented conscience at last tells him to release the Marquis, come what may. But why did Gauvain so decide?

The reason, though perhaps Hugo did not choose to admit it even to himself, might be expressed in two French words: *noblesse oblige*. Lantenac and Gauvin were two great gentlemen, endowed with what Burke called "the unbought grace of life," instructed from childhood to protect children and women. They acted selflessly out of habit and an inculcated sense of duty. Those two died for others; the Jacobin ex-priest killed himself out of devotion to an ideology. A reader of *Ninety-Three* may extract such a moral from the novel, even though Hugo did not intend to put it into his closing pages. For my part, reading *Ninety-Three* at the age of fourteen (as did Ayn Rand), I did unearth that moral, and ever since have given loyalty to persons precedence over loyalty to metaphysical politics.

Revolutionary though Hugo's sympathies were when he wrote *Ninety-Three*, this story is not really calculated to win converts to Jacobinism. The slaughter of the peasants of the Vendée was very like the liquidation of the kulaks of the Ukraine by the Bolsheviki, a hundred and thirty years later—and with the same excuse of thus providing for the welfare of a hypothetical posterity. Relatively few readers today are inclined to applaud the columns of troops sent into Brittany by Minos, Aecacus, and Rhadamanthus. (Hugo's father was among those soldiers of the Republic.) The inflammatory cry of "Liberty, equality, fraternity, or death!" rings somewhat false nowadays; one thinks of Pol

Pot, who returned to Cambodia after years at the coffee tables on the Left Bank of the Seine, and raised in his native land that Jacobin cry, and succeeded in destroying half the men, women, and children of Cambodia, through war, murder, or famine; and there the end is not yet. Better a Jacobite than a Jacobin.

Our third novel touching on the Armed Doctrine is less known than *A Tale of Two Cities* or *Ninety-Three*, but more skillful than either. I refer to Joseph Conrad's last complete novel, *The Rover*—of which the setting is the Mediterranean coast of France, near Toulon, during the years from 1793 to 1805.

The hero of this tale is a white-haired master gunner of the French navy (previously a Brother of the Coast, or virtual pirate, in the Indian Ocean), Peyrol. Home from the sea—he had been a waif on this shore, born into the lowest element of French rustic society—but still vigorous, and well supplied with gold, he finds lodging at a commodious farmhouse, Escampobar. The proprietress of the farm is a beautiful and fey girl, Arlette. At their first encounter in the farmhouse, she says to him, "Have you ever carried a woman's head on a pike?"

"No," the sea-fighter replies. "I have heard men boast of having done so. They were mostly braggarts with craven hearts. But what is all this to you?"

It is a good deal to Arlette of the black hair and the red lips; she may have carried a head on a pike herself; at any rate, she had run barefoot in blood, through the streets of Toulon when the English retreated and the sansculottes massacred the royalists. Her parents had been murdered there; then, first captive and later frantic participant, she had known all the horrors of those days and nights of the Terror at Toulon. In the end, she had been carried back to Escampobar by a sansculotte, who had been "busy purveying the guillotine," slayer perhaps of Arlette's parents, one of the drinkers of blood. Her sybilline aunt, Catherine, had prevented Scevola from making himself master of Arlette and the farm; but he lived with them still. "She is fit for no man's arms," said her aunt. That had begun in 1793.

On Peyrol's arrival, four years later, the Directory is in power, and France relatively calm. Arlette, after the exchange about heads and pikes, begins to finger the lapel of Peyrol's coat—"something that a child might have done." She tells him, " 'Yes. You may stay. I think we shall be friends. I'll tell you about the Revolution.' "

"At these words Peyrol, the man of violent deeds, felt something like a chill breath at the back of his head."

Stay he does, for eight years, during the time when Napoleon became First Consul and then Emperor. For the sake of those present who might read this novel for the first time, with pleasure, I refrain from recounting the plot. I will mention two episodes only, because they are relevant to the Armed Doctrine, revolutionary ideology. The first of these is Scevola's attempt to cut down the village priest with his saber; he finds it necessary to flee from a village mob, but is saved by the priest's intervention. The second is the heroic end of Peyrol—who sails out to sea in his little craft, for the sake of France and of Arlette and of her suitor, Lieutenant Real. Peyrol knows he will die under the guns of a British corvette; so he forces Scevola to accompany him, thus ridding the lovers of Escampobar, and France, of the sansculotte wretch whom Peyrol calls "a chicken-hearted spouter."

Conrad's detestation of his creature Scevola is the great novelist's final expression of contempt for radical ideologues—a theme which winds through his earlier novels *Nostromo, The Secret Agent, Under Western Eyes,* and some of his short stories. The stalwart pirate from the Indian Ocean is an angel of mercy by the side of murdering ideologues in red caps, those loitering patriots.

There runs through the pages of *The Rover* a certain weariness, which sometimes seems serenity. Peyrol rests after forty years of adventure at sea; France rests from the ghastly bloodshed of 1793; and Arlette, in love, gradually regains her sanity. The British fleet hangs off Toulon and Hyeres, as if anticipating Trafalgar; but the guns are silent for a time. The Revolution having devoured its children, France can breathe again.

Those three novels, and lesser ones, accomplished something to endow English-reading lands, at least, with a healthy prejudice against revolution and ideology. A later wave of books, chiefly by Russian writers of talent—Pasternak and Solzhenitsyn standing tall among them—has reinforced American and British distrust of belligerent schemes of perfectibility. There has been no American writer of any real merit, since Jack London, who has published novels of overturn—although certainly there was much radical or pseudo-radical scribbling in the land during the late 1960s and the early 1970s, most of it now thoroughly forgotten.

Nowadays we publish in this land a great mess of silly or disgusting fiction, but nothing of the literature of revolution—or nothing worth mentioning. Nearly forty years ago, Lionel Trilling expressed his hope that the intricacies of ideology might serve to revive the American novel; we have been spared that. Yet I should be mightily pleased if some talented man or woman should give us a novel, a really imaginative one, exposing the follies of ideological infatuation.

EQUALITY AS A FACTOR IN THE AMERICAN AND FRENCH REVOLUTIONS

STEPHEN J. TONSOR

Stephen J. Tonsor is a professor of history at the University of Michigan where he has taught since 1954. An adjunct scholar of the American Enterprise Institute and associate editor of Modern Age *for nearly two decades, Dr. Tonsor's areas of professional interest include European intellectual history, historiography, German socialism, and higher education. He is the author of* Transition and Reform in Education (*Open Court, 1974*), National Socialism: Conservative Reaction or Nihilist Revolt? (*Holt, Rinehart & Winston, 1959*) and dozens of articles and reviews in publications such as* Natural History, *the* Journal of Modern History, National Review, *the* New Catholic Encyclopedia, *and the* Christian Science Monitor.

THE NEW WORLD of the North American continent which so transformed European sensibilities and ideas in the three centuries from the discoveries to the American Revolution did so slowly, incompletely, and hesitantly. As is usually the case with those who confront a new situation, Europeans at first imposed their own ideas on experience. Only gradually did they accept the New World on its own terms and transform their society in a way which reflected their experience. The idea of equality was not born on the frontier. It came to the frontier together with many other European ideas which formed the intellectual baggage of the adventurers who first set foot on the North American continent. The New World environment served less to generate new ideas than to accelerate the development and deepen the notions Europeans brought with them from the Old World.

The society which Europeans brought to the New World was radically inequalitarian and hierarchical. In the Indian cultures which they first observed they thought they had found an equalitarian society. In fact they imposed their preconceived notions of mankind living in the golden age on the Indian cultures which they observed. The noble savage was invented not by incipient Romantics in the middle of the eighteenth century but by writers such as Montaigne who imposed the Stoic age of gold upon those children of nature they found living in the Brazilian jungles and the North American forests. It was a short-lived vision and Europeans imposed their differentiated social order as they imposed their religion on the indigenous populations. If equality had ever existed it was soon replaced by slavery.

Nor did the frontier transform the hierarchical society of Europe into an American model of freedom and equalitarianism. One need only study the divergent histories of Anglo-Saxon and Latin America, as Silvio Zavala suggests in his essay "The Frontiers of Hispanic America," to understand that it was culture rather than environment which determined the patterns of political and social development. The differing political and social fortunes of the North American and the Latin American peoples have been due to the survival of a culture European in origin and hierarchical in character in the Latin American instance. When revolution came to Latin America it was an equalitarianism based on the French-Revolutionary statist model rather than the Thomist-Lockean model.

To be sure, European hierarchical society was as much a

part of the social heritage of Anglo-Saxon and French North America as of Hispanic America. But it is very doubtful, says A. L. Burt, that this hierarchical society in North America can be described as feudal even in French North America. Robert Nisbet has argued that the American Revolution was an "equalitarian" revolution which aimed at the destruction of a "feudalism" imported into the North American colonies and in this respect hardly different from the French Revolution. Nisbet's argument is based on the attempt to import into North America the established churches, the legal institutions of primogeniture and entail, and the grant of truly feudal land patents—estates on the scale of Eastern Europe. Long before Nisbet, J. Franklin Jameson in *The American Revolution Considered as a Social Movement* had called attention to what he believed were the social implications of these huge landholdings. Though the "aristocracy" of New England was urban and mercantile rather than landholding, the manorial grants of New York, the huge holdings of the Penns, the Fairfax estate in Virginia which embraced six million acres, and the holdings of Lord Granville in North Carolina which included a third of the colony, seem to lend credence to this argument.

Only sociological abstraction and verbal legerdemain, however, can transform this system, even in Canada, into feudalism. On the eve of the American revolution 80 percent of the white males in the English colonies held property of sufficient money value to vote. The presence of an "established church" was no more feudal in the eighteenth century than it is in twentieth-century Britain. The easy availability of land and the development of yeoman proprietorships removed the possibility of feudalism in America north of the Rio Grande. Feudal patterns of landholding persisted in Hispanic America with social and political consequences which are still with us. Aristocracy and social hierarchy survived in the English colonies of North America but one can hardly call the social hierarchy of Boston or Philadelphia "feudal."

According to J. R. Pole in *The Pursuit of Equality in American History*, the most striking feature of the American colonial social scene was the evident contradiction between the confident reality of an increasingly equalitarian society and its hierarchical and aristocratic social and political forms. These forms endured until after the American Revolution. Moreover, says historian Gordon Wood, the change in form was not instigated by an equalitarian revolution from below but by a revolution from above.

Though property was widely held in colonial America, political participation was the exception rather than the rule. Government was left to the elites. Those aristocrats so brilliantly described by Carl Bridenbaugh in colonial Virginia had been prepared by birth and by training for the exercise of political leadership. Nor was this leadership contested by the lower orders. Indeed it was the competing elites who mobilized and energized the lower orders of society. Reluctant participation rather than an aggressive bid for political equality constituted the political reality on the eve of the American Revolution. It is, to a considerable extent, the Revolution which produces political equality rather than the bid for equality which produces the Revolution.

In the developing crisis from the 1750s to the outbreak of the Revolution just what was the nature of the appeal for "equality" on the part of so many English colonists in North America?

The first source of the quest for "equality" in colonial America was a major constitutional crisis within the British empire. While constitutional theory in England called for virtual representation, practice and theory in the American colonies were based upon actual representation. Americans argued that the Parliament at Westminster had no right to tax Britain's colonial subjects because the colonists had no representation in Parliament. Even Edmund Burke, that great and knowledgeable defender of colonial America, argued that the colonists were "virtually" represented in Parliament, that holders of a Parliamentary seat did not represent a specific geographic district or a specific constituency but rather represented the common interests of the realm at large. The American appeal was to equality of representation. This conception of actual representation has been of enormous force in American political life, for from it is ultimately derived the principle of "one man; one vote."

This principle was not an abstract idea which had no relationship to practical realities. Colonials knew they had been placed in a position of subordination in which their interests would be perennially sacrificed to the whim and welfare of the mother country. Constitutional "equality" was a matter of paramount importance. In *The Creation of the American Republic, 1776–1787*, Gordon Wood has observed that the American Revolution was not one but many revolutions. These varied grievances found unity of expression in the great constitutional crisis. The colonies were culturally, religiously, socially, and economically diverse; so diverse that it seems in retrospect astonishing that they could achieve the unity necessary to successfully establish a republic.

There was, however, more unity than was at first glance apparent. Socially there was far greater homogeneity than the prominence of social elites indicated. Something approaching equality, especially equality of opportunity, was the rule. America's "aristocracy" lived in modest eighteenth-century comfort rather than the grandeur of English lords and gentlemen. Even an Irishman rising in English political life, such as Edmund Burke, maintained a more lavish household than almost all American magnates. While it is true that the acreage of estates in America was impressive, it must be remembered that these lands were, for the most part, unimproved in a land of perennial labor scarcity. The aspiration to equality was, in fact, based on a social system in which the divergences of social class were being bridged. A society open to, and rewarding the achievements of, talent was already in existence. Colonial Americans thought of their society as essentially equalitarian and it was for this reason that they did not take the question of slavery and indentured servants very seriously. They respected wealth and achievement and were, being good eighteenth-century Englishmen, respectful of the elites. They aspired to status and honors and found these achievements in no way a contradiction to equality. They were opposed to entail and primogeniture because these were the legal institutions of hereditary aristocracy rather than an aristocracy of achievement.

Few factors were more important as a source of unity and a common political identity than the common law. The common law was case law developing in precedent to precedent. It was not statutory law although statutory law could affirm what common law had found. Indeed, it was argued in the troubled years preceding the American Revolution that where there was a conflict between statutory law and common law, the common law was superior and could control statutory law. This was the case because common law was a fundamental part of the English constitution.

When English kings issued general warrants for search and seizure in both America and England it was argued that they were behaving unconstitutionally. The first challenge to common law rights arose in Massachusetts shortly before a parallel case arose in England. Americans found themselves defending the constitution from what was perceived in both England and America as growing Hanoverian tyranny. "Writs of assistance" issued by the

Superior Court of Massachusetts on the authority of the reigning monarch and remaining in force throughout the lifetime of the monarch exempted customs offices from lawsuits and resistance when, in the course of collecting unpopular duties, they conducted searches of warehouses, stores, and private homes. When in 1763 John Wilkes, a member of Parliament, attacked the King and ministry, a decision was made to prosecute him for sedition, and a general warrant was issued to assist in searches to produce evidence. The desired evidence was discovered and Wilkes fled to the Continent. Edmund Burke played a leading role in defending his friend Wilkes and in helping to destroy what he viewed as the growing Hanoverian tyranny. Wilkes's case made its way through the King's courts and he was exonerated and general warrants were found to be illegal.

If general warrants were illegal in England, were they not also illegal in America? In 1767 Parliament passed the Townshend Act which imposed new tariffs on the colonies and at the same time legalized the writs of assistance and appointed courts in each colony to issue these general warrants. What Parliament in effect did was to establish one law for Britain and another for America, underlining the subordinate and unequal condition of the Colonies. Americans saw themselves not only struggling against inequality but fighting on the forefront in defense of the English constitution and the liberties of Englishmen. The common law became for them a school of liberty.

Moreover, colonial Americans had all studied the same political theorists. It is true, asserts Henry F. May, that the Enlightenment in America was as diverse as the Enlightenment in Europe. This diversity is represented by the writers quoted, and not always to the point, by American colonial pamphleteers on the eve of the Revolution, as Bernard Bailyn demonstrated. Still there is a unity rather than a unanimity of viewpoint in American colonial political theory. It is this unity which is reflected in the

Declaration of Independence and the U.S. Constitution. The American Revolution was a Lockean Revolution fashioned on the lines of the republicanism of the Commonwealth men. Locke and a republicanism derived from the radical Whig's reading of the ancient writers supplied the basic propositions of colonial political theory.

Locke's theory can hardly be described as a theory of radical equalitarianism. Morton Gabriel White has insisted, when Jefferson wrote in the Declaration of Independence, "We hold these truths to be self evident; that all men are created equal," he was quoting Locke, and nearly everyone who read him knew that he was quoting Locke. It will be recalled that Locke had written in *The Second Treatise on Government*, Chapter II, Section 4, that in the state of nature man is in:

> a state of equality, wherein all the power and jurisdiction is reciprocal, no one having more than another; there being nothing more evident than that creatures of the same species and rank, promiscuously born to all the same advantages of nature, and the use of the same faculties, should also be equal one amongst another without subordination or subjection, unless the Lord and Master of them all should by any manifest declaration of his will set one above another, and confer on him, by an evident and clear appointment, an undoubted right to dominion and sovereignty.

Both Locke and the Declaration of Independence seem, consequently, to give the most emphatic endorsement to the notion of a radical equality among men. The attribution of equality, however, is to the species not to the individual. All men have an equal right to liberty and consequently they are obliged because of this right to put no man under their dominion. Locke is not arguing, as Jefferson and the framers and signers of the Declaration of Independence were not arguing, "that all men are equal in

121

size, strength, understanding, figure, moral accomplishments, or civil accomplishments," as White, in *The Philosophy of the American Revolution* points out. It was clear to the founders, for example, that while women, as members of the species possessed rights and fell under obligations, they were, as were children, civically unequal. Even in the matter of "self-evident truths," Aquinas had held and Locke held after him that while these truths were evident to all men they were not apprehended by all men, not believed by all men. These "self-evident truths" are not innate but are rather apprehended by the reason. Some men may lack the acumen necessary for their apprehension. The reason of some men is clouded by vice and the passions. Some men are men of inferior capacities. Some men are to be characterized by the Theorist phrase, "invincibly ignorant." These men are, from a civil standpoint, unequal. They are incapable of distinguishing either those self-evident truths or the political obligations which follow from them.

The political theory of the founders was equalitarian rather than democratic. Though all are essentially and potentially equal not all are equally capable of civic participation. Property qualifications for political participation are not only commonplace but are philosophically justified as essential to a stable political order.

Given the wide distribution of property in colonial America, fears that the propertyless would, through the ballot, redistribute wealth and expropriate the property-holders was not widespread. Having read the Roman historians, colonial political theorists had other fears. They recalled that wealthy Romans based their power on the clientage of the poor and the landless. Jefferson's fears of a landless proletariate, urban and engaged in manufacturing, stem from the same source. The great enemy of republican institutions was not the poor but rather the rich, the aristocracy, who mobilized the poor to the political advantage of the aristocracy. These fears had their origins not only in the political experience of ancient Rome but in the contemporary reality of English party politics. Political dependency is seen as the great enemy of liberty and independence. Property qualification for political participation, inequalitarian though it was, was not too high a price to pay for the preservation of republican political institutions.

Political corruption, tyranny, and a systematic attack on the English constitution were the charges made by the Whigs against the royal government in both England and America. These radical Whigs believed that the tyrant achieves his objective through corrupting men with luxury. Luxury is the great enemy of liberty.

In 1734, Thomas Gordon, a well-to-do radical Whig who published assiduously throughout his lifetime, produced *The Works of Sallust Translated into English with Political Discourses upon that Author.* Gordon had previously published a similar translation and commentary on *The Works of Tacitus* in 1728. In spite of the fact that Gordon was wealthy and well-connected he clearly believed that despotism and luxury went hand in hand. In Section IV, page 98 of his translation and commentary on Sallust, he writes:

> such is the Nature of Man, and of Society, that wherever the means of corruption are found, the Exercise of it will soon follow. *Rome* was at first virtuous from Necessity, very Poor, almost always in War and Danger. Poverty, and Equality (which is often the Effect of Poverty, especially in new Establishments, before the pride of Blood and Lineage begins) proved her Defense for some time against Ambition. She had no Trade, no Money, no Room or Materials for Luxury. Temperance and Frugality naturally followed Necessity. Iron, the best Instrument in forming and preserving their State was more esteemed than Gold, which men seldom love, till it has hurt them; taught

them by Use or Desire more than they want. They had no Slavish Dependents; for the Relation of Patron and Client implied no more than a kind Intercourse of Protection and Duty. Bach supported Himself; for none were able to support Many, and thence to draw numerous Dependencies. Liberty was their great Passion; Virtue had all the opportunities of shining, none of being debauched and enervated. But their Habits changed with their Condition; they first grew less Virtuous, then Vicious, at length abandoned. It is the Course and Fate not of *Romans* only, but of Men.

Gordon's works are a tissue of such passages. He strengthened an ancient argument and made it applicable to present conditions. Like other Commonwealth men, he had his eye upon the France of Louis XIV. More obviously he felt the Hanoverian monarchs and their ministers were corrupting English republican virtue, enslaving men with luxury and reducing free-born Englishmen to the status of minions of a tyrant. Caroline Robbins has produced a number of studies to suggest that Gordon was only one of many radical Whigs who appealed from present politics to ancient example. Gordon was also, according to Bernard Bailyn, very widely read in America and the situation of the colonies was seen through his eyes. The colonists' fears were not that tyranny would make the achievement of equality impossible but rather that an already achieved equality would be smothered by luxury and tyranny. They made a revolution not in the name of equality to be gained but rather in the name of equality to be retained.

It is difficult to say just when the Revolution began in America. Certainly it was underway long before the Declaration of Independence. John Adams' letter of 1815 to Thomas Jefferson on this matter is often quoted:

What do we mean by the Revolution? The war? That was no part of the Revolution; it was only an effect and consequences of it. The Revolution was in the minds of the people, and this was effected, from 1760 to 1775, in the course of fifteen years before a drop of blood was shed at Lexington.

In the last generation it was popular to interpret the American Revolution as a class conflict based on what were assumed to be the "real" and "objective" factors of historical causation. Much of that crude and simplistic material-social interpretation has now been dissipated and the weight of the evidence suggests agreement with Bernard Bailyn's "rather old-fashioned view that the American Revolution was above all else an ideological, constitutional, political struggle and not primarily a controversy between social groups undertaken to force changes in the organization of the society or the economy." The objective of the Revolution was not the achievement of an equalitarian society. It does not follow from this, however, that the revolutionary ideology locked the young republic into a status quo society. In the years which immediately followed the Revolution the full implications of that revolutionary ideology manifested themselves. By the time Alexis de Tocqueville visited the United States in 1831–32 it was clear that equality was the great pivotal force in American society. One is tempted to argue as John Henry Newman argued in his *Essay on the Development of Christian Doctrine* that in the course of history that which is implicit and *in potentia* in any body of doctrine will manifest itself in a fully developed form.

That the American Revolution was not a revolution made to transform the social and political structure of society becomes increasingly clear when we compare it to that other great contemporary upheaval, the French Revolution.

The comparison of these two revolutions has been the ideological dividing line of modern historical studies. It is tempting to trace an ascending revolutionary arc which begins at Lexington and Concord, breaks over the walls of the Bastille, and culminates in the Bolshevik revolution of 1917. This interpretation of the revolutionary movements that have supposedly characterized the onset of modernity itself, becomes an ideological weapon to be employed in the triumphant forward march of the proletariate. The romance of the revolution is the last great romantic enthusiasm. It is not difficult, therefore, to understand why the historians of the left should wish to link these three great revolutions. The effort, however, has never been successful.

Even when the American and French Revolutions are seen from a non-ideological perspective, the perspective of "democratic revolution," the effort to find common elements and a common program, says R. R. Palmer in *The Age of Democratic Revolution*, dilutes the distinctive character of both revolutions. That the American Revolution played an influential role in the development of the revolutionary spirit in Europe is undeniable. Even so, that influence ought not to be overestimated. The financial debts France incurred in the course of intervening in the American Revolution were probably more important in sparking the revolution in France than were the revolutionary ideas and example of America.

These two revolutions are as different and distinctive as any two events in the history of the modern period. Those living close on these events were often aware of their difference. It is sometimes asked by those who have not studied him carefully why Edmund Burke so eloquently defended the embattled American colonists and was so outraged at the course of the revolution in France. Burke's differing attitude to these two events is usually ascribed to the fact that he had grown old, reactionary, embittered, and disappointed in the years between the two revolutions and was unable to bring to the French Revolution the generous understanding which characterized his attitude

126

to the American colonies. It is hardly possible to misunderstand more completely Burke's thinking and motives.

Burke had studied the history and situation of the American colonies as had few Englishmen of his day. Any topic which engaged his interest became the subject of his exhaustive enquiry and if Burke knew America from study, he knew France at first hand. In both cases Burke was prepared to make the most able political judgment of his time on the events which unfolded in America and in France and he found these events radically different in character.

It must be remembered that Burke spoke from a Whig revolutionary experience and from an Irish perspective. Change consonant with the constitution, extending the rights inherent in the constitution, in keeping with historical experience and tradition and grounded in prudence and prejudice seemed no revolution at all to Burke. When Americans appealed to the Crown, Parliament, and the world on the basis of their rights as Englishmen, Burke could only applaud and warn his fellow members of Parliament of the dangers of an imprudent lack of sensitivity. The appeal of the Americans, whether they were right or wrong, was to the constitution and tradition.

In the French instance Burke found the opposite to be the case, according to Gerald Chapman's *The Practical Imagination*. The causes and the course of the French Revolution were not dictated by ancient tradition and established rights, by prudence and prejudice, but by the abstract theories of rationalist *philosophes*. Burke did not deny the validity of natural rights but commented that their "abstract perfection was their practical defect." It was these men, according to Burke, who determined the course of the Revolution. Thomas Carlyle popularized Burke's explanation in his *History of the French Revolution*. Twentieth century intellectuals have usually derided this explanation as simplistic and farfetched, but Burke was probably right in assessing the influence of the *philos-*

ophes. François Furet has argued in *Interpreting the French Revolution* that in the pre-revolutionary period the thought of Rousseau played an enormous preparatory role. Furet reasserts, "His political thought set up well in advance the conceptual framework of what was to become Jacobinism and the language of the Revolution. . . ." The failure of the established elites to provide reformist leadership in the years immediately before the revolution permitted this power to devolve on the *philosophes.* Furet writes:

> That is why eighteenth-century society turned to other spokesmen, namely to the *philosophes* and men of letters. . . . That confusion of roles, in which men of letters assumed a function they could fulfil only in its imaginary aspects, that is, as opinion-makers who wielded no practical power whatsoever, was to shape political culture itself. The men of letters tended to substitute abstract right for the consideration of facts, principles for the weighing of means, values and goals for power and action. . . .

It is these ideas through their own internal dynamic which provide the vocabulary of revolution and develop through a process of internal radicalization. Central to the system was the Rousseauian notion of equality.

Burke was not alone in his insight. Friedrich Gentz, later secretary to Metternich, had translated Burke's *Reflections on the Revolution in France* and was thoroughly familiar with Burke's argument. In April and May of 1800, Gentz published in the *Berlin Historisches Journal, The French and American Revolutions Compared.* The young John Quincy Adams, then resident in Prussia, translated the Gentz pamphlet into English. Gentz was absolutely correct in observing that the American Revolution had "more the appearance of a foreign, than a civil war." Whereas in America there was little attention to the equalization of status and no attack on property, in France the opposite was the case.

> How infinitely different was in this point of view the situation in France: If the French Revolution had been content merely to destroy with violent hands the old constitution, without making any attack upon the rights and possessions of private persons, it would, however, have been contrary to the interest of a numerous, and in every respect important class of people, who by the sudden dissolution of the old form of Government, having lost their offices, their incomes, their estimation and their whole civil existence, would of themselves have formed a powerful opposition—But, when in its further progress, it no longer spared any private right whatsoever, when it declared all political prerogatives to be usurpations, deprived the nobility not only of their real privileges, but likewise of their rank and title, robbed the clergy of their possessions, of their influence, and even of their external dignity; by arbitrary laws took from the holders of estates half their revenues; by incessant breaches of the rights of property, converted property itself into an uncertain, equivocal, narrowly straitened enjoyment, by recognizing publicly principles of the most dangerous tendency, held the sword over the head of everyone, who had any thing to lose, and aggravated the essential wretchedness, which it everywhere spread by the ridicule and contempt it shed over every thing that bore the name of possessions, or privileges—then truly it could not fail to accumulate against itself a mass of resistance, which was not to be subdued by ordinary means.

France's constitutional and fiscal crises were the immediate and necessary cause of the French Revolution, but the sufficient cause lay in the realm of ideology. For nearly a century the heirs of Hobbes, Louis XIV, and, more recently, Rousseau, had been preparing a revolution that would usher in a centralized and autocratic state, govern in the name of the people, deny any transcendent purpose to man's existence, and create a political world based upon a thoroughgoing equality. In short, the ideology of the French Revolution was radically different from that of the American Revolution. (Just how different they were becomes clear in *John Adams and the Prophets of Progress* by Zoltan Haraszti, which cites the notes and marginalia with which John Adams embroidered the pages of Mary Wollstonecraft's *The French Revolution.*)

The intellectual groundwork for the French Revolution had been laid for a long time. The first major figure in a tradition which reaches through Gracchus Babeuf to Karl Marx is Jean Meslier (1678–1729). Meslier's revolutionary transformation of society is based upon the murder of God and the abandonment of any idea of transcendence. The abolition of ideas of human essence and the substitution of a conception of nature wholly without purpose or teleological direction opens up the possibility of a world subject to change and transformation in accordance with man's needs and purposes.

The achievement of absolute human equality would seem to necessitate the destruction of God and the abandonment of the transcendent, for it is in these notions that the hierarchical structures of society are rooted. Meslier's substitution of the "order of nature" for the order of God has this objective in view. Meslier believed present society to be unnatural because it is premised on inequality. Communism is the order of human society. Property must be held in common and common labor takes the place of essential humanity, defines the human essence. The current political regime must be overthrown because it is based on inequality of status and inequality of consumption. Reason and the "order of nature" are to be

130

substituted for the order of God and the false society takes its rise from property.

There is hardly a memorable or profound thought in the works of this typical representative of the first age of cocktail-party metaphysics. His notions are typical of the intellectual culture of the academies, lodges, and salons of eighteenth-century France. Like other metaphysical and anthropological quacks of the eighteenth and later centuries his ideas would long ago have been swept into the capacious dustbin of history had it not been for the fact that the later revolutionary socialists all derive a considerable fund of their ideas from Meslier.

There are many echoes of Meslier in the writer we know as Morelly. We know, indeed, very little of him beyond his name and his works, attributed in his lifetime to Denis Diderot. When Gracchus Babeuf first read Morelly he believed he was reading Diderot. *The Code de la Nature* of 1755 is the key text. Unlike Meslier, Morelly believed the force of reason so powerful that it unaided would overthrow an unjust and unnatural society without the need of revolutionary violence. Moreover, he sees no need for the destruction of God as called for by Meslier. God is simply banished to the Deistic role of prime-mover, the conservator of order and harmony in the universe. God is a *deus absconditus*, a God who has disappeared from the world, impersonal and unknowable. "Nature" is the determinant of order. The transcendent disappears; life after death has no meaning and life's purposes are the satisfaction of natural appetites. Society is a collectivity in which mankind as a whole achieves its fulfillment in relation to nature.

The division of labor, the passions of man, and the common ownership of property provide the cement of the social collectivity. All of these factors lead to a natural innocence in the achievement of human satisfactions.

Morelly's problem was that of so many of his "philosophic" contemporaries. If nature is ordered and harmonious, and man because he is continuous with nature, good, how then do evil and confusion enter into human society? Since the idea of sin, and particularly the notion of original sin, has been banished there would seem to be no explanation. The explanation lies in error, false reasoning which corrupts the whole of society and brings with it degree, property, and priestcraft. Only through right reasoning can these errors be corrected and a perfected mankind living in a perfected society be put in its place. To the larger question of how the good man in the natural order could reason falsely, Morelly has no answer.

As Morelly is an important contributor to the literature of revolutionary social transformation it is well to weigh the elements to be found in his work and to note those which are absent. As with the theorists of socialism generally there is a thoroughgoing denunciation of the present state of human society, a society whose evils are a direct consequence of the presence of degree, property, and inequality of condition. These are by definition found to be unnatural and unreasonable. Although Morelly is a Deist he is hostile to all religious orthodoxy which he sees as "priestcraft" and which he believes to be an important element in man's enslavement. Morelly is not, however, a theorist of alienation and he does not explain man's present condition in economic terms. Finally, Morelly does not argue for a progressivist historicist developmental pattern of stages which make reason immanent in history.

There are important points at which the philosopher Condillac's brother, the Abbé Gabriel Bonnot de Mably, disagrees with both Meslier and Morelly. Mably's equalitarianism as expressed in his voluminous works made him the most widely known and read socialist theorist of the prerevolutionary period.

Equality is the "natural order of society." It is an order of nature fixed neither by the physical need for natural satisfactions nor the division of labor but rather by the moral demands of man's reason and feelings. It is an ideal to be actualized rather than a reflection of physical determinants. There once was a state of nature, still reflected in the lives and societies of noble savages in America and Africa, in which these rational ideals of socialist society were realized. The restoration of harmony in society can be achieved by returning to these ideal conditions. Mably speaks eloquently of reason, but, like his contemporary Rousseau, he emphasizes feeling. With Mably as with Morelly the decay of men and institutions is initiated by inequality and unequal property. Only the rational reconstruction of society on a socialist basis can restore the lost social harmony.

On the eve of the French Revolution, French social theorists Meslier, Morelly, Mably, Rousseau, and Diderot desired the reconstruction of society on an equalitarian model. They called repeatedly and loudly for a lawgiver, a Lycurgus, Solon, or Plato who would through wise legislation provide a model socialist society like that of Plato's Republic. It is this ideology of equality which makes the French Revolution so different from the American.

Like the American Revolution, the French Revolution had taken place in the minds of men before it eventuated in the streets of Paris. Before the Oath of the Tennis Court and the fall of the Bastille the revolution had already triumphed. The idea of equality was its most dynamic radicalizing force. The abolition of hierarchy, degree, status, and privilege was an inevitable development which followed in the wake of the revolutionary ideology. That power should drift steadily and inevitably to the left in the assembly was implicit in the ideas which dominated the Revolution. That property should be attacked and that the economic "liberalism" of the intellectuals should gradually give way to populist equalitarianism and the legislated distributism that characterized the republic of virtue assumes the force of historical inevitability.

The republic of virtue dominated by Robespierre enacted in terrible form the equalitarian pseudo-Spartanism of Rousseau. Historical experience underlines the fact that a state with such a socio-political configuration cannot exist aside from the systematic application of terror. Robespierre's Republic of Virtue has this in common with Pol Pot and the Khmer Rouge. While it is true that the Robespierrean republic of virtue did not attempt to enact a socialist program, it was, in fact, socialism piecemeal; the sort of program Huey Long might have enacted had he become President of the United States.

The Thermidorian reaction and the execution of Robespierre were also inevitable. Revolutionary fervor and systematic terror can maintain themselves at fever pitch only so long. Reality will break in. July 1794 suppressed the Rousseauist Spartan state but it could not suppress the ideology and political factions which had dominated the republic of virtue. Out of power, and being a conspiratorial and large minority, these revolutionary extremists plotted their return to dominance in the state.

The man who formulated the ultimate implications of equalitarian revolution was Gracchus Babeuf (1760–1797). In the interregnum between the republic of virtue and the establishment of the Napoleonic tyranny it was Babeuf and his fellow conspirators who dreamed of turning the clock back and rejuvenating the Revolution. Babeuf had taken part in the republic of virtue and, imprisoned and brooding on past glory, he not only dreamed of a revolutionary restoration but sought to give revolutionary principles a new and more trenchant formulation. For the first time in history, Babeuf argues for the necessity, if revolutionary movements are to be successful, of a revolutionary conspiratorial elite, a cadre of professional revolutionaries.

Moreover, the socialism which was piecemeal in the republic of virtue is now given a systematic formulation. Babeuf had studied Rousseau, Meslier, and Morelly. He too denounced property and the commercial system. The new social and economic system was one to be based on the socialist "order of nature." In the new society there would be neither money nor trade. All would contribute the fruits of their labor to the "common storehouse." There would be a national network of workshops and storehouses and from these every citizen would receive "every necessary object of consumption." Those who were invalided or who were too young or too old to participate in the labor force would be supported by society.

> Everything will be blended together and on a footing of perfect equality: producers who are agricultural-ists and workers who follow a trade, artists and scientists, storekeepers, allocators and distributors responsible for getting material products to the consumers. All distinctions between industry and commerce will disappear, and there will be a fusion of all professions raised to the same level of honor. . . .

Babeuf's socialism has a religious flavor. He wishes to found "the holy league of the equality of the common happiness." The conspiratorial revolution will abolish all government. Crime and exploitation of every description will disappear and mankind will be enabled to achieve a perfect happiness.

It was easier to write about than to achieve perfect happiness. True, an elaborate conspiracy was organized. The Insurrectional Committee was endlessly busy. In the spring of 1796 the plans for a revolution were fully developed. The police, however, were informed and Babeuf and the chief conspirators arrested. Efforts to carry through the revolution ended in a brief flurry of riot which was easily suppressed. Babeuf came to trial in the spring of 1797 and was found guilty. Twenty hours after a botched attempt to stab himself, Babeuf was executed.

The chief beneficiary of the "conspiracy of equals" and the encroachment of anarchy was Napoleon Bonaparte.

Edmund Burke, long before the advent of the Corsican general, saw clearly the consequence of the decay of hierarchy, the confusion of orders and the quest for equality. He knew that the deposition of the King and the abrogation of the constitution would lead to military tyranny. Burke wrote:

> In the weakness of one kind of authority, and in the fluctuation of all, the officers of an army will remain for some time mutinous and full of faction, until some popular general, who understands the art of conciliating the soldiery, and who possesses the true spirit of command, shall draw the eyes of all men upon himself. Armies will obey him on his personal account. There is no other way of securing military obedience in this state of things. But the moment in which that event shall happen, the person who really commands the army is your master; the master (that is little) of your king, the master of your assembly, the master of your whole republic.

However, when all other differences have been eradicated, all other grades leveled, all hierarchies dissolved there will remain the differences of biology and the supposed differences of race. In discussing the impact of equality on the French Revolution, the Swiss diplomat and historian Carl J. Burckhardt notes:

> Once Napoleon I when the causes of the French Revolution were being endlessly discussed in his presence ended this discussion with the observation, "It was much simpler: the brunettes killed the blondes." This opinion introduced a richly developed biological-historical explanation in the course of whose development Gobineau distinguished himself and which then at the level of the half-educated in the extraordinary exaggeration of our century was transposed into real events.

Napoleon's observation, in spite of the anti-Frank, Philo-Roman currents present in the French Revolution, was less a description of what had been than it was a description of what was to be. When inequality ceased to be a matter of status or of wealth it became a matter of race.

INFLATION AND CONTROLS IN REVOLUTIONARY FRANCE: THE POLITICAL ECONOMY OF THE FRENCH REVOLUTION

RICHARD M. EBELING

Richard M. Ebeling holds the Ludwig von Mises chair in economics at Hillsdale College. Educated at California State University, Rutgers University, and the National University of Ireland at Cork, he is well-known as one of the nation's leading Misesian scholars and free market advocates. A former assistant professor of economics at the University of Dallas, he joined the Hillsdale faculty in 1988. He is on the editorial board of the Review of Austrian Economics *and is vice president for academic affairs for* The Future of Freedom Foundation. *The author of the forthcoming book,* A History of Austrian Economic Thought *(Croom-Hill, Ltd.), Professor Ebeling has also published thirty articles and more than a dozen reviews.*

O̲URS HAS BEEN the century of the total state. When, in the 1920s, Benito Mussolini coined the term "total-itarian," he captured the spirit of the age. In no other period in man's history have so many human beings been sacrificed on an altar engraved with the words, "For Reasons of State." Millions have been treated as refuse fit only for disposal in ovens. Tens of millions have been starved to death, worked to death, tortured to death in the cause of constructing utopias on a grand scale. For most of our century, over large portions of the earth, humane behavior towards one's fellow man has been the bestowing of death with a bullet to the back of the neck.

Nor is it surprising that war in our century has often been total war. In an epoch in which the distinction between society and the state has been blurred at the minimum and erased in the extreme, "The Enemy" is no longer the ruler and his army of hired professionals, as it was in the Middle Ages—an earlier age in which all sides followed an etiquette of war, in which the status of noncombatant was recognized and his life and property were meant to be respected. In the total state the individual has no existence outside of his role and function within the collective plan. He and everything he possesses is the property of the state to which he belongs. Victory in war, in such a world, requires the combatants to view all those who live and work on the other side of the battleline as "The Enemy," because all who live and work across that line do so at the command of the opposing state. To defeat the enemy requires the destruction of the people in the opposing state and all that they have or could produce.

In the total state, therefore, the concept of private property loses its meaning. Even if property has not been nationalized, even if individuals are not meticulously regulated at every moment in every detail of their economic activities, the logic of this system is that at any moment, for any purpose, the individual, his property, and his productive energy are at the unreserved disposal of the state. Life and property are at the liberty of the state.

As we approach the end of the twentieth century, the age of the total state seems to be coming to a close. The trauma and destruction of the two world wars have faded into memory. The decline of the collectivist ideal, even in socialist countries, makes it appear that the worst has been past. The twenty-first century may indeed be an era of limited and free government, a period of individual liberty and free market prosperity. But it is worth recalling that at the beginning of the twentieth century there were few seers who expected these hundred years to turn out the way they have. The belief then, too, was that the future would herald nothing but expanded freedom and increasing prosperity. After all, the thinkers of 1900 argued, we learned the lessons of the French Revolution and in the nineteenth century we created in its place civilized regimes based on a sense of humanity and a respect for the individual and his rights to life and property; the twentieth century would merely provide improvements on this liberal ideal. Our century is proof that the men of 1900 were wrong. Not all the lessons that the French Revolution could teach were learned, and, what was worse, some of the lessons that had been learned in the nineteenth century were forgotten in the twentieth.

Among the lessons forgotten were those that economics can teach. Almost every one of the mistakes and disasters that we have experienced with economic policy in our own times were applied and experimented with during the French Revolution: deficit spending; regulation of private enterprise; nationalization of property; wage and price controls; and inflationary destruction of the monetary system.

But if the French Revolution is to be an object lesson in bad economics, its prologue is in the policies of the Old Regime. Imbued with the spirit of mercantilism, the royal French government believed it was responsible for regulating and overseeing all the economic activities of France. From imports and exports to production and investment and the pricing of commodities, the state concerned itself with everything. There is no better guide for a brief summary of the patterns of royal regulation than Alexis de Tocqueville. In his book, *The Old Regime and the French Revolution,* all the pertinent details are spread before the interested reader. A few passages will give the necessary flavor of the period:

> Orders were passed prohibiting the cultivation of this or that agricultural produce in lands which the Council [the economic authority in Paris] considered unsuited to it. Others required that vines planted in what the Council regarded as bad soil should be up-rooted. To such an extent had the government exchanged the duties of sovereign for those of guardian.
>
> The government had a hand in the management of all the cities in the kingdom, great and small. It was consulted on all subjects, and gave opinions on all; it even regulated festivals. It was the government which gave orders for public rejoicing, fireworks, and illuminations.
>
> The church, which a storm had unroofed, or the presbytery wall which was falling to pieces, could not be repaired without a decree of Council. This rule applied with equal force to all parishes, however distant from the capital. I have seen a petition from a parish to the Council praying to be allowed to spend twenty-five livres.
>
> A very extensive machinery was requisite before the government could know everything and manage everything in Paris. The amount of documents filed were enormous, and the slowness with which public business was transacted such that I have been unable to discover any case in which a village obtained permission to raise its church steeple or repair its presbytery in less than a year. Generally speaking, two or three years lapsed before such petitions were granted.
>
> Nobody expected to succeed in any enterprise unless the state helped them. Farmers, who, as a class, are generally stubborn and indocile, were led to be-

lieve that the backwardness of agriculture was due to the lack of advice and aid from the government.

Government having assumed the place of Providence, people naturally invoked its aid for their private wants. Heaps of petitions were received from persons who wanted their petty private ends served, always for the public good.

To quote one more authority, the French classical liberal, Charles Dunoyer, from his book, *The Passage to Liberty*:

The state exercised over manufacturing industry the most unlimited and arbitrary jurisdiction. It disposed without scruple of the resources of manufacturers; it decided who should be allowed to work, what things it should be permitted to make, what materials should be employed, what processes followed, what forms should be given to productions. It was not enough to do well, to do better; it was necessary to do according to the rules.

And while the King's Council regulated the economic affairs of his subjects, the King's Court consumed the national wealth. Louis XVI's military guard numbered 9,050 persons; his civil household numbered around 4,000—thirty servants were required to serve the King his dinner, four of whom had the task of filling the King's glass with water or wine. The King had 1,857 horses, 217 vehicles, and 1,458 men in liveries. In 1786 there were 150 pages in the palace, 128 musicians, 75 religious officials, 48 doctors and assistants, 383 officers of the table, 103 waiters, and 198 persons for the personal domestic services of the King.

To pay for this extravagance and the numerous other expenses of the Court, as well as the foreign adventures financed by the King (such as the financial help extended to the American colonists in their war for independence against the British), the King had to rely on a peculiar tax system in which large segments of the entire population—primarily the nobility and the clergy—were exempt from all taxation, with the "lower classes" bearing the brunt of the burden. One of the most hated of the taxes was the levy on salt. Every head of a household was required to purchase annually seven pounds of salt for each member of his family at a price fixed by the government; if he failed to consume all the salt purchased during the previous year and, therefore, attempted to buy less than the quota in the new year he was charged a special fine by the state. The punishments for smuggling salt and selling salt on the black market were stiff and inhumane.

The discrepancy between what the royal government spent and what it collected in taxes was such that at the time of Louis XVI's accession to the throne in 1774 the accumulated royal debt was 2,470,000,000 livres, (a livre then being worth about 20 cents). The expenses for that year alone were 399,200,000 livres, with tax receipts of only 371,980,000 livres, leaving a deficit of 27,220,000 livres. Loans had made up the difference in the past and would continue to be used in the future.

But out of this regulatory and fiscal madness, France was given the opportunity for economic redemption. The new King appointed Anne Robert Jacques Turgot as controller of the finances. A follower of the Physiocrats, an articulate proponent of free trade and *laissez-faire*, Turgot had been a brilliant administrator of one of the French provinces and brought it increased prosperity by establishing a general free market policy in the area under his jurisdiction. As finance minister of the entire country, Turgot now instituted an economic revolution: He abolished all grain tariffs between the provinces of France; he abolished the practice of forced labor for road building and other public works; and then he abolished the trade guilds and the government-protected manufacturing monopolies. And he declared that the royal deficits would be solved through cuts in government spending and not through an increase in taxes.

But every lowering of a tariff, every elimination of a trade guild, every removal of a monopoly privilege, increased the array of special interest groups determined to defeat Turgot. Their chance came with the King's recall of Parliament, for here was their opportunity to veto Turgot's free market reforms and protect their privileges and monopolies. And on May 12, 1776, the King dismissed Turgot under the pressure of the special interests. Thus France's one chance before the Revolution to establish an economic regime of free markets at home and free trade abroad was lost.

Those who followed Turgot as controller of the nation's finances lacked his vision or integrity. The fiscal crisis merely grew worse and worse. As Thomas Carlyle summarized it in his study of *The French Revolution*:

> Be it "want of fiscal genius," or some far other want, there is the palpablest discrepancy between Revenue and Expenditure; a *Deficit* of the Revenue. . . . This is the stern problem: hopeless seemingly as squaring the circle. Controller Joly de Fleury, who succeeded Necker, could do nothing with it; nothing but propose loans, which were tardily filled up; impose new taxes, unproductive of money, productive of clamor and discontent. As little could Controller d'Ormesson do, or even less; for if Joly maintained himself beyond a year and a day, D'Ormesson reckons only by the months. . . . Fatal paralysis invades the social movement; clouds of blindness or of blackness envelop us; are we breaking down then, into the black horrors of NATIONAL BANKRUPTCY?

It was the royal finances that was the immediate cause for the calling of the Estates-General at the beginning of 1789. And it was the chaos of the two months following the fall of the Bastille in July 1789, that set the stage for the beginning of the economic policies of revolutionary France. In the words of the Italian historian, Guglielmo Ferrero, in his work, *The Principles of Power*:

> All over France . . . [t]he majority was carried away by an unaccountable frenzy, the minority followed willingly or unwillingly, convinced up to a certain point only; but the fact remains that everyone revolted. Barracks and monasteries were emptied as soldiers and monks deserted, the army scattered to the four winds, the administration was dislocated, neither courts nor police functioned any longer, taxes and seignorial dues were no longer paid, everywhere monasteries and castles were stormed and pillaged . . . in a few weeks . . . [t]he aristocratic and monarchic hierarchy . . . vanished into nothingness, disappeared into an enormous crevasse of history that all at once opened up beneath its age-old foundations.

In August the French National Assembly was told that practically no taxes had been collected for three months—and this at a time when more than 160,000 livres a month were being spent in Paris alone for the creation of public works jobs; and this following a spring during which the National Assembly had "lent" the people of Paris almost 17,000,000 livres out of the national treasury to buy food.

In November 1789, Mirabeau proposed an answer to all of the government's financial difficulties. In the previous month, the National Assembly had nationalized all the estates and properties of the Church. Mirabeau now suggested that paper notes be issued by the National Assembly with the Church lands as collateral. The notes would first pass into circulation as spending for public works and other expenses of the government. They would be redeemable at face value in the form of purchase price for Church property. At the same time, it was argued, the added circulation would give a stimulus to industry, create jobs, and put money in the pockets of the working classes. (Later it would be the confiscated lands of the nobility who had fled France that would be used as the fictitious collateral behind a flood of paper money.)

On March 17, 1790, the National Assembly voted for the issuance of the *assignats*, as the paper notes were called. And the first issue was released in April in the amount of 400 million livres. But by the end of the summer the government was again short of funds and 800 million more assignats were printed. The arguments for issuing these additional quantities of paper money had to overcome the fears of some in the Assembly that the prosperity that the proponents of the *assignats* spoke of would only lead to the destructive forces of inflation. But the Assembly was swayed by the appeal of Mirabeau, once again, that only the bankers and capitalists might be harmed, and their interests were not those of France.

Andrew Dickson White points out in his classic monograph on *Fiat Money Inflation in France* that the first issues of the *assignats* were passed by the Assembly only with great difficulty, because of a fear and reluctance to risk the monetary stability of France. But having once tried the forbidden fruit, it became increasingly easy for the government to go back for more, and more. And with increasing regularity the Assembly did. In his famous study of *The Assignats*, Seymour Harris divided the history of the paper money into six periods, in which he estimated the quantities of the *assignats* in circulation and their decrease in value. But it is sufficient to look at these numbers at the beginning, the middle, and the end of their history. At the end of 1791, 1,490,000,000 livres were in circulation and during these first two years of their existence their market value had depreciated, in terms of their buying power against goods, by 14 percent. By August 1793, there were now 4,050,000,000 livres in circulation; their value, in terms of their buying power against goods, had depreciated by 60 percent. And by November 1795, total *assignats* in circulation had risen to 19,700,000,000 livres, with their buying power in terms of goods having diminished by 99 percent from 1790. In a matter of five years, the revolutionary money of France had become worth less than the paper upon which it was printed.

The effects of this monetary collapse upon the society were fantastic. A huge debtor class was created that had a vested interest in the continuation of the inflation, because every worsening of inflation meant that they paid back their debts in increasingly worthless money. Others had used the *assignats* to purchase former Church or aristocrats' land, and their fortunes were now dependent upon inflationary rises in land values; the lure of larger and larger monetary profits to be reaped during the inflation lead to vast speculative transactions. Nothing was important, anymore, other than the pleasures and opportunities of the moment. Heinrich von Sybel, in his four-volume *History of the French Revolution*, writes:

> None felt any confidence in the future in any respect; few dared to make business investment for any length of time, and it was accounted a folly to curtail the pleasures of the moment, to acquire or save for an uncertain future. . . . Whoever possessed a handful of *assignats* or silver coins, hastened to spend them in keen enjoyment, and the eager desire to catch at every passing pleasure filled each heart with pulsations. In the autumn all the theatres had been reopened, and were frequented with untiring zeal. . . . The cabarets and cafes were no less filled than the theatres. Evening after evening every quarter of the city resounded with music and dancing. . . . These enjoyments, too, received a peculiar coloring—glaring lights and gloomy shadows—from the recollections and feelings of the Revolution. . . . In other circles no

one was received who had not lost a relative by the
guillotine; the fashionable ball-dress imitiated the
cropped hair and the turned-back collar of those who
were led to execution; and the gentlemen challenged
their partners to the dance with a peculiar nod, intended to remind them of the fall of the severed head.

As inflation grew worse, everything became higher in
price and scarcer in supply. In 1793, soap had become so
scarce that the washerwomen of Paris demanded that merchants who refused to sell soap for *assignats* should be put
to death. Andrew Dickson White recounts that

on February 28, 1793, at eight o'clock in the evening,
a mob of men and women in disguise began plunder-
ing the stores and shops of Paris. At first they demanded only bread; soon they insisted on coffee and
rice and sugar; at last they seized everything on
which they could lay their hands—cloth, clothing,
groceries, and luxuries of every kind. Two hundred
such places were plundered. This was endured for six
hours, and finally order was restored only by a grant
of seven million francs to buy off the mob.

Nor did the promised inflationary prosperity of the inflation last very long. To quote White again, "Under the
universal doubt and discouragement, commerce and
manufacturing were checked or destroyed. As a consequence, the demand for labor was stopped; laboring men
were thrown out of employment, and, under the operation
of the simplest law of supply and demand, the price of
labor—the daily wages of the laboring class—went
down. . . ."

On whom did the major burden of the inflation ultimately fall? None other than those in whose name the
inflation was introduced: the working classes. The
wealthy, the financiers, the merchants who dealt in inter-

national trade had both the means and often the opportunity to protect themselves from the ravage of the inflation. They hoarded gold and silver or sent their supply of specie aboard; they invested in art or precious jewels. Their speculative expertise enabled many of them to stay ahead of inflation and gain from currency movements. The working classes had neither the means nor the knowledge to protect themselves. "On them finally came the great, crushing weight of the loss," as the *assignats* ended up left in their hands the more the inflation ran its course.

Finally, on December 22, 1795, it was decreed that the printing of the *assignats* would end. Gold and silver transactions were permitted again and recognized as legally binding. And on February 18, 1796, at nine o'clock in the morning, the printing presses, and the plates and paper used in the printing of the *assignats* were taken to the Place Vendome and before a huge crowd of Parisians the means for making paper money were broken and burned.

But the inflation of the *assignats* was only one part of the economics of revolutionary France. With the Jacobin's accession to power in 1792, the rest of the policies soon fell into place. The collectivist vision of the Jacobins submerged the individual into the body of the nation. The individual had no existence outside the nation. "The Republic must penetrate the souls of citizens through all the senses," declared Barere in 1794. The individual's life, his work, his very being belonged to the nation. A year earlier Barere had made this very clear:

> Some owe [France] her industry, others their fortune; some their advice, others their arms; all owe her their blood. Thus, then, all French people of both sexes and of all ages are called upon by *la patrie* to defend liberty. . . . Let everyone take his post in the national and military movement that is in preparation. The young men will fight; the married men will forge arms, transport baggage and artillery, and provide

subsistence; the women will work at the soldiers' clothing, make tents, and become nurses in the hospitals for the wounded; the children will make lint out of linen; and the old men, again performing the mission they had among the ancients, will be carried to the public squares, there to enflame the courage of the young warriors and propagate the hatred of kings and the unity of the republic. The houses of the nation shall be turned into barracks, the public squares into workshops, the cellars into factories of gunpowder.

All laws, customs, habits, modes of commerce, thought, and language were to be uniform and the same for all. Not even the family had autonomous existence; and children? They belonged to the state. "The principles that ought to guide parents are that children belong to the general family, to the Republic, before they belong to particular families," insisted Barere. "The spirit of private families must disappear when the great family calls. You are born for the Republic and not for the pride or the despotism of families."

The Jacobin view of economics should not be surprising. To quote Barere once more:

The vice we ought to cure in this country is the versatility of principles of political economy.... What we need is a system of national works, on a grand scale, over the whole territory of the Republic.

In the winter of 1791–92, prices in France began to rise significantly, partly due to the effect of the flooding of the economy with the *assignats* and partly due to a bad harvest in 1791. When war was declared on Austria on April 20, 1792, cries were heard for price controls on commodities and for government regulation of industry and commerce. Standing before the National Assembly on April

25, 1793, as representative of the Committee of Agriculture and Commerce, Boudin declared, "No individual has exclusive rights to the fruits of the earth. . . . All citizens have equal rights to the products of the earth upon paying a just indemnity to those who cultivate it." He recommended to the Assembly that a "maximum price" be placed on grain. Santerre assured the Assembly that the high price of grain was due merely to the avarice of merchants and farmers.

On May 4, 1793, the price control on grain was passed, with the further regulation that all grain was to be sold only in public markets; severe penalties were imposed at the same time for all illegal dealings. "All merchants, cultivators, and proprietors of grain and flour shall be required to declare, at the municipal bureau nearest their homes, the quantity and nature of their grains and flours and, by approximation, the quantity of unthreshed grain in their possession," declared the new law. "Directors of districts shall name commissioners in the divers municipalities to observe the execution of this measure." The municipal authorities were given the power to arrest "speculators" and "hoarders" and permitted to enter the homes of any citizens suspected of fraudulent declarations. Confiscated grain and flour were to be distributed to the poor at no charge.

Farmers rapidly and creatively found ways to evade the new law. Fearing that the price controls would spread to other parts of the economy, the prices of other goods rose. The hoarding of grain became widespread; to counter this, the Assembly made forestalling a capital offense on July 26, 1793. Even the destruction of any commodities under the price controls was declared to be a capital offense. Public warehouses were established to guarantee government supervision of grain and its sale. On August 19, the controls were extended to firewood, coal, peat, and pit coal. And finally, on September 29, 1793, the General Maximum was passed, placing all commodities of "primary necessity" under the price control regulation. All prices were to be fixed at no higher than one-third higher than their 1790 level.

Commodities soon disappeared from the markets. Paris cafés found it impossible to obtain sugar; food decreased in supply everywhere as farmers refused to send their produce to the cities. The American economist, Edwin Kemmerer, in his study of the economics of the French Revolution, explained some of the ways the controls were evaded:

> Among the methods employed for evading this price-fixing system the following may be cited: the withdrawal of goods from the market and the failure to produce new supplies when the existing stocks were exhausted; the production and sale of inferior quality; the feeding of grain to farm animals at times when the prices of grain were subject to the Maximum and the prices of live animals were not; the milling of wheat into flour by the farmers when the price of wheat was controlled and the price of flour was not. Farmers sold their produce at home clandestinely, instead of bringing it to market. When the prices of raw materials were controlled, the price of manufactured articles frequently rose abnormally, and, when the prices of necessities were held down, the prices of luxuries soared. Evasion of the law yielded large profits, while the penalties for evasion, if one were caught, were extreme. This led to much official corruption. The supply of goods available in the markets at the controlled prices were often inadequate and the queue, as in Russian cities of today, became a familiar institution.

Nor were wages free from the supervision and control of the state. In the spring of 1794, tobacco workers demanded and were refused an increase in their pay. A week later, similar demands were made by transportation workers; they were told that their labor had been requisitioned by the state. Bakers were warned that wage demands on their part would place them in the category of "suspected" persons—sufficient grounds to face the guillotine.

Only on December 27, 1794, was the Price Maximum finally repealed. By this time the anti-Jacobin Thermidorians had the upper hand. The advocates of the market economy were able to make their case. On December 7, for example, Eschasseriaux delivered a speech before the Assembly in which he concluded:

> A system of economy is good when true principles are spread throughout a state and when people have confidence in their execution; when work and the products of the earth are regarded as the primary wealth of the nation; when national prosperity rests upon the two primary bases of all prosperity, agriculture and commerce; when the farmer, the manufacturer, and the trader enjoy the full liberty of their property, their production, and their industry.

He was joined by Thibaudeau:

> I regard the Maximum as disastrous, as the source of all the misfortunes we have experienced. It has opened a career for thieves, covered France with a hoard of smugglers, and ruined honest men who respect the law. I know that unlimited liberty can cause the greatest of inconveniences, but I also know that, while you violate commercial liberty, you are subjected to even greater inconveniences. I know that when the government attempts to regulate everything, all is lost.

During the Jacobin Republic of 1792–94 a swarm of regulators had spread across France imposing price ceilings and intruding into every corner of people's lives; they imposed death sentences, confiscated wealth and property, and sent men, women, and children to prison and slave labor. In the name of the war effort all industries in any way related to national defense or foreign trade were put under the direct control of the state; the prices, production, and distribution of all these private enterprises were under the direct command of the state. A huge government bureaucracy emerged to manage all of this, and that bureaucracy swallowed increasing portions of the nation's wealth.

All of it followed naturally from the premises of the Jacobin mind. Under the shadow of Rousseau's notion of a "General Will" that can never be wrong and always reflects the true interest of the nation as a whole, it was inevitable that those who could know that "General Will" and truth would see it their duty—and their "right"—to impose it on France. Those who did not see the General Will would be taught; those who refused to accept after the teaching would be commanded; and those who resisted would perish, because only "The Enemy" would oppose.

The individual was nothing, the state was everything. The individual became the abstraction, and the state became the reality. And all were consumed in this bonfire of the insanities.

But why did the Revolution fail? Why did the people, in whose name all this had been done, constantly frustrate and resist those who were establishing the "new order"? The answer, I would like to suggest, had been given by Adam Smith thirty years before the Revolution in his first book, *The Theory of Moral Sentiments.* It is found in his analysis of "the man of system," the social engineer and planner who desires to remake society in his own image:

> The man of system ... is apt to be very wise in his own conceit, and is often so enamored with the sup-

posed beauty of his own plan of government, that he cannot suffer the smallest deviation from any part of it. He goes on to establish it completely and in all its parts, without regard either to the great interests or to the strong prejudices which may oppose it; he seems to imagine that he can arrange the different members of a great society with as much ease as the hand arranges the different pieces upon a chess-board; he does not consider that the pieces upon the chess-board have no other principle of motion besides that which the hand impresses upon them; but that, in the great chess-board of human society, every single piece has a principle of motion of its own, altogether different from that which the legislature might choose to impression upon it. If those two principles coincide and act in the same direction, the game of society will go on easily and harmoniously, and is very likely to be happy and successful. If they are opposite or different, the game will go on miserably, and the society must be at all times in the highest degree of disorder.

Each individual possesses a spirit and a purpose of his own. The planner, the social engineer wishes only one spirit and one purpose to manifest itself in the world—*his own*. But, the human spirit is greater than all the power of the planner, even when he possesses the terror of the state. Each man attempts to discover his own destiny, to fulfill his own life and to make it better as he conceives it.

The beauty of the free society and its market order, as Adam Smith so brilliantly demonstrated in 1776, in his *Wealth of Nations*, is that when governments recognize the sanctity of the individual, and respect peaceful competition and voluntary exchange among free men, then the two principles of social order and liberty coincide. Each individual "engineers" his own life, and, as by an invisible hand, each in his own endeavors often serves the common good.

If, in our reflections on the events in France two hundred years ago, we relearn the important distinctions between state and society, between the peaceful order of the market and the terror of state command, between the imposed will of one and the free wills of all, then the French Revolution will be a warning and a guide for the decisions we must face in the next century.

THE FRENCH REVOLUTION AND MODERNITY

KENDALL W. BROWN

An associate professor of history at Hillsdale College, Kendall W. Brown has also served on the faculty of the University of North Carolina at Charlotte, Duke University, and the Universidade Federal de Santa Catarina in Brazil. Dr. Brown is the author of nearly a dozen articles and book chapters as well as Bourbons and Brandy: Imperial Reform in Eighteenth-Century Arequipa *(University of New Mexico Press, 1986) and co-author of* Peru, *the first volume in* The Royal Treasures of the Spanish Empire in America *three-volume series (Duke University Press, 1982). His scholarship has focused on royal absolutism and state-building. At Hillsdale, he teaches "The Age of Enlightenment," which includes a section on the French Revolution.*

THESE ESSAYS COMMEMORATE the bicentennial of the French Revolution. Some have raised the question of whether that momentous series of events fulfilled its promise. Even to attempt an answer to that question would require us to distill out of the Revolution exactly what its promises were, assuming that it embodied some and that we could agree on what they were. In so doing we would be well served to keep in mind the storms of controversy which have surrounded the Revolution, both during the years it was unfolding and in the two centuries since. William Wordsworth wrote of the early Revolution:

"Bliss was it in that dawn to be alive, / But to be young was very heaven!" On the other hand, writing in the early nineteenth century, conservative historian Hippolyte Taine called the Revolution an "insurrection of donkeys and horses against men, under the leadership of monkeys with parrots' tongues." With opinion thus ranging from heaven to hell, we ought to tread cautiously as we examine the historical evidence of the Revolution and ask ourselves, as did J. M. Thompson, was the Revolution "the 'suicide of the eighteenth century'," or "the birth of ideas that enlightened the nineteenth, and of hopes that still inspire our own age"?

My purpose here is not the hunt for promises but the search for meaning: What did the French Revolution mean? What did the revolutionaries think it meant? What did it mean for the future, particularly as it concerned European and Western civilization? The contributors to this volume have used a number of symbols to give meaning to the Revolution, ranging from the guillotine to Rousseau to the Terror. We have even had the whole affair laid at the door of the Marquis de Sade. In another place and with a different audience there would undoubtedly be more talk of the idealism of the *sansculottes*; of Robespierre, the Incorruptible, trying to establish the Republic of Virtue; of a foreshadowing of the Russian Revolution and the ultimate triumph of socialism or Marxian communism.

The French Revolution means many things for the present age. For example, it bequeathed us French *haute cuisine*. With the onset of the Revolution, chefs who had previously toiled in the kitchens of the aristocracy found it necessary to open restaurants. Competing for diners, says Richard Cobb, they invented an ever-expanding number of flavorful sauces and dishes and established the fame of French food throughout the world. Cobb also notes that the Revolution enriched our political vocabulary. Among other examples, "left" and "right," have their modern connotations because radicals tended to sit to the left of the president of the National Assembly and reactionaries on the right. The Revolution also created a new type of huge national army, officered by the middle class rather than the nobility. With its highly motivated soldiers, such an army could resort to mobile and offensive tactics that Old Regime forces found impossible. The French Revolution also dealt a death blow to monarchy. In the Western world, divine-right absolutism expired when the revolutionaries forced Louis XVI to abandon Versailles and move to Paris in October 1789. Whereas before the Revolution, Tocqueville remarks, "the King's subjects felt toward him both the natural love of children for their father and the awe properly due to God alone," that sacrosanct nature of monarchy died with the trial and execution of Louis XVI. While there were still monarchs, even in France, after Louis's death, Michael Walzer concludes in an article on the monarchy, "the magic of kingship was never restored." The ideology of the Revolution had destroyed its mythological role.

But such examples of the Revolution's influence really fail to get at its impact upon modernity. If by "modernity" we simply mean a time more recent than the past, our use of the term reveals our bias for and preoccupation with the present. But modernity also refers to a series of social, economic, political, and intellectual changes in Western culture which have come to dominate the present age. First, Western man no longer conceives of society as a divinely instituted and permanent hierarchy in which some men are by birth superior to others. In the Old Regime, says Robert Darnton, "most people assumed that men were unequal, that inequality was a good thing, and that it conformed to the hierarchical order built into nature by God himself." At the very least, popular opinion today would consider such ideas bizarre and more likely racist or sexist. Instead, modern society holds that "all men are created equal." This idea of natural equality does not mean, according to the French historian François Furet, "that all men are born equal in strength or intelligence, but that no one has the right to subject others, since every person is endowed with sufficient reason to obey only himself," an appealing but dubious assumption.

If modernity believes in equality, it also holds liberty dear. In Old Regime society, privilege dependent upon birth or corporate status, defined liberty. For example, a French nobleman enjoyed freedom from certain taxes because he was a member of the privileged estate of nobility. But modern opinion holds that since all men are capable of reason, they should enjoy the liberty of obeying only themselves. To avoid the anarchy inherent in such liberty, however, two general political philosophies evolved to guide man's liberty. One held that man should behave according to self-interest but subject to a higher power such as market forces or an enlightened ruler. The other, most fully expressed by Jean-Jacques Rousseau's concept of the general will, posited that society can avoid anarchy and turmoil only if free individuals commit themselves first to the common good.

Allied with liberty and equality in the modern world is a belief in progress. For the past two centuries, man has confidently assumed that through science, technology, and industrialization, he can control nature, expand economic benefits, and modify society, although the greenhouse effect, fears about nuclear power, and burgeoning Third World poverty have given cause for more pessimism. Liberty has seemed to assure continuing economic progress through the elimination of mercantilistic and monopolistic practices inherited from the Old Regime, such as royal companies, craft guilds, and commercial prohibitions.

What did the French Revolution have to do with these characteristics of modernity? The French Revolution was a gate through which the Western world passed into modernity. It was not the only passageway; neither did it

160

represent a clean break with the past and a jump-start on modernity. But the Revolution took pre-existing conditions and ideas which had been developing, particularly since the mid-1700s, passed them through a cataclysm, and changed forever the way humanity saw society, religion, the state, and the nation. The Revolution seared "Liberty, Equality, and Fraternity" into the consciousness of Western man, and ever since we have been wrestling with political, social, and economic experiments which aim to make all people free and equal, bound together by the ties of universal brotherhood. In the words of Furet, the Revolution gave the world "a haunting vision," its "first experiment with [modern, secular] democracy."

Despite attempts in the early months of the Revolution to establish a constitutional monarchy, the French predilection for equality and opposition to the privileges associated with Old Regime society were obvious from the summer of 1789. By August of that year, the Old Regime was gone, demolished by decrees of the National Assembly. Its edict of August 11 abolished the feudal rights of the nobility. As Alexis de Tocqueville concluded: "The French nobility had stubbornly held aloof from the other classes and had succeeded in getting themselves exempted from most of their duties to the community, fondly imagining they could keep their lofty status while evading its obligations. . . . They led nobody; they were alone, and when an attack was launched on them, their sole recourse was flight." Then on August 26, the National Assembly promulgated the Declaration of the Rights of Man and of the Citizen, intending it as the preamble to the constitution which they were to write. Whereas the decrees abolishing feudalism had resolved that no one was superior by birth, the Declaration explicitly established political and social liberty and equality: "Men are born and remain free and equal in rights," it stated. "Social distinctions can be based only on public utility."

For Tocqueville, the Revolution thus gave vent to two

French passions. One was a "deeply rooted," "indomitable hatred of inequality": "a desire, inveterate and uncontrollable, utterly to destroy all such institutions as had survived from the Middle Ages and, having cleared the ground, to build up a new society in which men were as much alike and their status as equal as was possible, allowing for the innate differences between individuals." The other passion was hunger for liberty.

These passions unleashed tremendous creative energy, whose aim was nothing less, Tocqueville claims, than the regeneration of mankind. Fraternity would reign among free and equal men. Perhaps nowhere was the revolutionary fervor and idealism better illustrated than in the Constituent Assembly on July 7, 1792. Factions within the Assembly engaged in bitter debate, paralyzing the body's deliberations and generating more and more animosity. Finally, a delegate named Lamourette rose to speak. He blamed all controversies on factionalism and said that what the revolutionaries needed was more fraternity. Robert Darnton recounts the memorable scene, "Whereupon the deputies, who had been at each other's throats a moment earlier, rose to their feet and started hugging and kissing each other as if their political divisions could be swept away in a wave of brotherly love." Dispute and controversy had momentarily given way before an emotional and naïve faith in the power of fraternity, yet we should not underestimate the force of that belief.

It turned the Revolution into what Tocqueville called a parallel of a religious revolution, a strange paradox in light of the revolutionaries' attacks upon the French church. "The French Revolution aspired to be world-wide and its effect was to erase all the old national frontiers from the map. . . . It created a common intellectual fatherland whose citizenship was open to men of every nationality and in which racial distinctions were obliterated." Jefferson wrote "all men are created equal" but kept his slaves in bondage; the French revolutionaries abolished slavery.

Thus, part of what the Revolution contributed to modernity was its universal slogan of "liberty, equality, and fraternity." These concepts had been evolving during the Enlightenment, but the revolutionary upheaval, according to Darnton, "created a new sense of possibility—not just of writing constitutions nor of legislating liberty and equality, but of living by the most difficult of revolutionary values, the brotherhood of man." Frenchmen of the 1790s believed that mankind was malleable, that men could change the entire course of history through the violent exertion of revolutionary will. Support for these principles was widespread. In the Assembly's debate over the Declaration of the Rights of Man and of the Citizen, little opposition emerged and that from only a few clergy because it weakened the privileged position of the Church.

The revolutionaries' faith in human reason, borne of the Enlightenment, gave them confidence that their ideals could be achieved. Reason made it possible to know the answers to revolutionary problems and devise political solutions. This optimism regarding human reason and the possibility of using it to create a new, democratic man was certainly part of the Revolution's legacy to modernity. All the democratic revolutions of the nineteenth century were, in one way or another, echoes of what began in 1789 France.

Another contribution of the Revolution to modernity was political centralization. Old-Regime France was a mish-mash of overlapping jurisdictions, competing officials, unequal taxation, and privileged groups. Despite the monarchy's attempts to centralize its hold over the country, it had not succeeded in eliminating these challenges to its authority. Building on the centralization begun under royal absolutism, the Revolution swept away the political vestiges of feudalism and eliminated the discrepancy between France's unequal institutions and the growing democratic spirit. Tocqueville, in fact, sees such centralization as one of the principal consequences of democracy: whereas the nobility had managed to stave off the Crown's program of concentrating power, the Revolution swept away the aristocracy and thus removed any brake on the tendency toward centralization. It thus provided the bridge between the absolute monarchy of Louis XVI and the Napoleonic state.

That bridge was the modern secular state, in which the government replaced the Church as the ultimate authority on social behavior and law. Albert Soboul has written, "The Revolution destroyed the *ancien régime*'s absolutist state, which had been based on the theory of divine right and which had guaranteed the privileges of the aristocracy. In its place, it set a liberal and secular state, based on the principles of national sovereignty and civil equality." This state followed lines suggested by the French Physiocrats: an impersonal bureaucracy with limitless authority and rights. Such a state had the power to subordinate the individual to the general will, in a society in which all citizens were absolutely equal. Of course, the need to make all citizens equal, to force adherence to the general will, made such a democracy even more centralist, because only a strong central government had the power to carry through the requisite radical political and social restructuring.

But as the revolutionaries discovered and as the world learned from France's experience, it was one thing to talk about reconciling freedom with equality through such a state but quite another to accomplish the task. When the obstacles to such reconciliation mounted, the Revolution became more radical, more violent, and more terrible. Although the Revolution's partisans believed it would produce a "new man," says Mona Ozouf, endowed with liberty and equality, some perceived obstacles to this regeneration: supporters of the "old man" and the Old Regime, especially priests, would attempt to prevent it. This turned the political arena of revolutionary France, in Furet's words, into a "realm of truth and falsehood, of good and evil." Framed in such ideological terms, those who resisted the Revolution were not mere political opponents but traitors to self-evident political solutions knowable through reason. How could anyone oppose liberty, equality, popular sovereignty, and fraternity, asked the revolutionary spokesmen. The reasonableness of these revolutionary values was self-evident. Those who opposed them did so not from mistaken logic but from malice and evil intent. Thus, adds Walzer, "the world was divided into friends and foes of the Republic, the People, and the enemies of the People, and once the enemies were identified, it was hardly necessary to prove their guilt. What was necessary was to kill them."

In a provocative and insightful interpretation, Furet refers to these real or imagined threats as the "aristocratic plot" and argues that the fear of such a plot energized France to defend the revolutionary values. "The aristocratic plot . . . was the notion that mobilised men's convictions and beliefs, and made it possible at every point to elaborate an interpretation and justification of what had happened." Parisian crowds stormed the Bastille to seize gunpowder when rumors spread that the Crown was sending troops against the city. From July to August 1789, the Great Fear convulsed rural France, with the countryside convinced that the nobility had armed hordes of brigands and beggars to terrorize the peasantry. In 1792, with Prussian armies triumphant in the field and the threat of treachery mounting at home, Parisian mobs massacred half the prison population of the city, horribly mutilating and butchering recalcitrant priests, aristocrats, and even common criminals.

In such ideological upheaval, the institution of the Church, if not belief in God, consequently came to be perceived as an enemy of the Revolution. The Church's great wealth and vast landholdings made it one of the socio-economic pillars of the Old Regime. It represented authority, tradition, privilege, and hierarchy. These contradicted the revolutionaries' catechism of human reason, progress, equality, and popular sovereignty. The irreligiosity of the French aristocracy and intellectuals prior to the Revolution created an atmosphere of skepticism and anti-clericalism which played into the hands of the radicals once the Old Regime collapsed.

The violence of the Revolution is difficult for us to appreciate and understand. On the one hand, the revolutionary tribunals and vigilante justice exterminated some 30,000 to 40,000 people, a mere trifle compared to the millions slaughtered by twentieth-century political extremists. In fact, sources like Henry Kammen provide figures which lead us to conclude that it was perhaps twice the number of French Protestants butchered in the St. Bartholomew's Day Massacre, only a little more than the English killed for witchcraft during the 1600s, and far less than the Germans liquidated for the same reason. Nor should we forget that people of the 1790s were more accustomed to violence than we who carry out our executions hidden from public view. Apologists for the guillotine and the political trials are also quick to point out that many executions occurred during times of great peril, when the pressure of foreign armies whipped the French into hysteria. But in the September massacre of 1792, the French reverted temporarily to inexcusable, primordial horror. They raped women and hacked off their breasts, used naked corpses for tables and chairs, and drank the blood of victims. It was hardly enlightenment in the realm of reason. And the Great Terror of June and July 1794, actually occurred after the threat from abroad had diminished. Madame Roland reportedly looked up at a statue erected to symbolize Liberty just before being executed and exclaimed: "Oh Liberty, what crimes are committed in your name!"

More clearly than anyone, the revolutionary leader Brissot expressed the dynamic of the aristocratic plot: "The

traitors will be convicted in the end, they will be pun-
ished, and we shall finally be able to get rid of everything
that prevents France from becoming a great nation. I admit, gentlemen, to only one fear, namely, that we may not
be betrayed. . . . We need great acts of treason: therein lies
our salvation. . . . Great acts of treason will be fatal only to
those who perpetrate them; they will serve mankind." In
other words, the leaders could rally the people to the cause
most effectively by discovering and revealing conspiracies
against the people's revolution. At the same time, the
unearthing of such plots conveniently enhanced the
power of the leaders.

Thus every leader from Mirabeau to Lafayette to Robespierre faced the dilemma of consolidating power despite
accusations by even more radical groups who claimed to
have uncovered plots against the Revolution. The *sansculottes*, the Parisian working class, were passionately
egalitarian and demanded that the government use any
repressive measures necessary to combat threats to social
and economic equality. Anyone voicing a contrary opinion was immediately accused of being involved in an aristocratic plot. It was extremely difficult, if not impossible,
to reject these allegations because they were the lifeblood
of the revolutionary ideology. Yet to give in to the accusations meant instituting the Terror to combat the Revolution's internal foes and waging war against its external
monarchical enemies.

In the maelstrom of the Revolution, the leaders were too
weak to resist such pressure, even when they were so
inclined. This was true in theory because revolutionary
ideology had enshrined the people as sovereign. It was true
in practical terms because the revolutionaries feared executive authority and were unwilling to invest a single individual with such power. We think of Robespierre as being
despotic, and some Parisians called him a tyrant when he
fell. But even Robespierre lacked centralized executive
power, which lay divided among the members of the Na-

tional Assembly or between the members of the executive committees appointed by the Convention. His authority came from his position on the Committee of Public Safety, which he shared with eleven other men; from his oratory; and from his ability to embody better than anyone else not only the sentiment of the Convention but also the revolutionary spirit of the people. But when popular opinion and the Convention turned against Robespierre, the guillotine claimed him.

With power so divided and so tenuously held, it raised the question of who really represented the popular or general will, a question which democratic regimes have been attempting to answer for the past two hundred years. Even though the people had elected the delegates to the Convention, the *sections* of Paris, the Jacobin clubs, and the radical press also claimed to voice the opinion of the people. Acting on its own initiative on November 23, 1793, for example, the Commune, or municipal government, of Paris closed all churches in the city to the consternation of most members of the Committee of Public Safety and particularly Robespierre. While the French had by and large either supported or accepted the confiscation of Church property and establishment of the Constitutional Church, those were attacks upon a religious institution rather than open warfare upon religion and God. Robespierre, says Alfred Cobban, "was too good a Rousseauist in his religious ideas not to see behind dechristianization the sinister shade of atheism." These unofficial watchdogs not only dug to discover anti-revolutionary plots but scrutinized the actions and statements of the government leaders for adherence to revolutionary orthodoxy. From 1789 to the emergence of Napoleon, no individual or group permanently established its legitimacy as an embodiment of the general will. And for that reason political turmoil continued because power seemed available.

Soboul notes that such energy, idealism, and violence

fed off each other to produce what Marx called the "terrible hammer-blows" and "giant's broom" which destroyed pre-revolutionary society and swept it away. When the Old Regime collapsed in the spring and summer of 1789, it left an ideological vacuum which the revolutionaries tried to fill, according to Tocqueville, with "broad generalizations, cut-and-dried legislative systems, and a pedantic symmetry." Centuries-old traditions gave way before abstract theories which enshrined liberty and equality. This was modernity, bursting from the long gestation of the scientific revolution and the Enlightenment. Like a gigantic child, the Revolution knew no bounds. Its naïve faith in the regeneration of humanity through revolutionary doctrine foundered on the hard facts of reality. Man and his society proved less malleable than the revolutionaries anticipated, and their social engineering demonstrated the dangers of radicalism. J. L. Talmon has written of the French Revolution that it confirmed "the incompatibility of the idea of an all-embracing and all-solving creed with liberty. . . . To attempt to satisfy both at the same time is bound to result, if not in unmitigated tyranny and serfdom, at least in the monumental hypocrisy and self-deception which are the concomitants of totalitarian democracy." Even Robert Darnton, more sympathetic than Talmon to the French Revolution writes, "The Terror *was* terrible. It pointed the way toward totalitarianism. It was the trauma that scarred modern history at its birth."

But it would be unfair to claim that the French Revolution was the first step along an inevitable road leading to the Russian Revolution and Stalinism, just as it would be wrong to assert that it was inexorably leading to a new, secular Utopia. To blame all the evils of modernity on the French Revolution is to give it more credit than it deserves. It glosses over the crucial role, for instance, of Karl Marx who devised an ideology which subordinated philosophical speculation to the need for action to achieve the predestined materialist Utopia of communism. By focusing upon the evils of the Terror, we also overlook the regrettable mistakes of the Old Regime leaders. The King, aristocracy, and Church enjoyed the privileges of that society. Perhaps rather than according them our sympathy for having lost their heads, we ought to question their failure to use them.

The French Revolution did reveal, however, the contradictions and conflicts inherent in the basic assumptions which undergird modernity. Like us, the French declared man free to obey himself, guided by his own reason. They detested the feudal order which bound man to a fixed place in the social hierarchy. Like us, the revolutionaries admired equality before the law and popular sovereignty. For better or worse, the French Revolution originated the centralized, secular democratic state, a creation not far removed from the current United States of America, although our Constitution wisely divides power to prevent the tyranny of the legislature. We are more skeptical than Robespierre and Saint Just about the possibilities of social engineering, but the French revolutionaries lacked our 200 years of perspective to dampen their naïve enthusiasm. So what did the French Revolution have to do with modernity? It had to do with the question of whether we can be free and equal beings, bound together in a secular democracy and living in universal brotherhood. Modern man doesn't know the answer, but he keeps posing the question.

SELECT BIBLIOGRAPHY

Bailyn, Bernard. *The Ideological Origins of the American Revolution.* Cambridge: Harvard University Press, 1967.

Betto, Frei. *Fidel and Religion.* New York: Simon & Schuster, 1987.

Billington, James H. *Librarian of Congress's Remarks on the Occasion of the Millenium of Russian Christianity.* n.d.

Billington, James H. *Fire in the Minds of Men.* New York: Basic Books, 1980.

Billington, Ray Allen. *Land of Savagery, Land of Promise: The European Image of the American Frontier in the 19th Century.* New York: W. W. Norton & Co., 1981.

Bridenbaugh, Carl. *Seat of Empire: The Political Role of 18th-Century Williamsburg.* Charlottesville: University of Virginia Press, 1963.

Brinton, Clarence Crane. *The Anatomy of Revolution.* New York: Vintage Books, 1965.

Brinton, Clarence Crane. *The Jacobins: An Essay in the New History.* New York: New York, Russell & Russell, 1961.

Burckhardt, Carl J. "Bei Befrachtung von Desmoulins Denkmal," *Begegungen.* Zurich: Manesse Verlag, 1958.

Burke, Edmund. *Reflections on the French Revolution in France,* ed., Conor Cruise O'Brien. Harmondsworth: Penguin Books, 1969.

Burt, A. L. "If Turner Had Looked at Canada, Australia and New Zealand When He Wrote About the West," *The Frontier in Perspective,* eds. Walker D. Wyman and Clifton B. Kroeber. Madison: University of Wisconsin Press, 1965.

Carlyle, Thomas. *The French Revolution: A History.* Chapman & Hall, 1863.

Chapman, Gerald W. *Edmund Burke: The Practical Imagination.* Cambridge: Harvard University Press, 1967.

Chesterton, G.K. *A Handful of Authors: Essays on Books and Writers*, ed. Dorothy Collins. New York: Sheed & Ward, 1953.

Cobb, Richard, ed. *Voices of the French Revolution.* (n.p., 1988).

Cobban, Alfred. *A History of Modern France*, 3 vols. New York: Braziller, 1965.

Conrad, Joseph. *The Rover.* New York: Doubleday & Co., 1923.

Darnton, Robert. "The French Revolution—What It Really Meant," *New York Review of Books.* (Jan. 19, 1989).

Dawson, Christopher. *The Gods of Revolution.* New York: New York University Press, 1972.

Dickens, Charles. *A Tale of Two Cities.* Harmondsworth: Penguin Books, 1981.

Doyle, William. *Origins of the French Revolution*, 2nd ed. New York: Oxford University Press, 1988.

Dunoyer, Charles. *The Passage to Liberty.* n.d.

Ferrero, Guglielmo. *The Principles of Power: The Great Political Crises of History.* Westport: Greenwood Press, 1984.

Furet, Francois. *Interpreting the French Revolution*, trans. Elborg Forster. Cambridge: Cambridge University Press, 1981.

Gay, Peter. *The Enlightenment, An Interpretation: The Rise of Modern Paganism.* New York: Vintage Books, 1966.

Gay, Peter. *The Party of Humanity.* New York: W. W. Norton & Co., 1971.

Gentz, Friedrich. *Three Revolutions: The French and American Revolutions Compared*, trans. John Quincy Adams, and *Reflections on the Russian Revolution*, by Stephen Possony. Washington, DC: Regnery Gateway, 1990.

Gershoy, Leo. *The French Revolution and Napoleon.* New York: Meredith Publishing Co., 1964.

Gordon, Thomas. *The Works of Sallust Translated into English With Political Discourses Upon the Author.* (n.p., 1734)

Haraszti, Zoltan. *John Adams and the Prophets of Progress: A Study of the Intellectual and Political History of the 18th Century.* Cambridge: Harvard University Press, 1952.

Hibbert, Christopher. *The Days of the French Revolution.* New York: William Morrow, 1980.

Honour, Hugh. *The New Golden Land: European Images of America From the Discoveries to the Present Time.* New York: Pantheon Books, 1975.

Hugo, Victor. *Ninety-Three*, trans. Helen E. Dole. New York: T. Y. Crowell & Co., 1888.

Jameson, Franklin J. *The American Revolution Considered as a Social Movement*. Princeton: Princeton University Press, 1926.

Kamen, Henry. *The Spanish Inquisition*. New York: New American Library, 1966.

Kuehnelt-Leddihn, Erik Ritter von. *Leftism: From Sade and Marx to Hitler and Pol Pot*. Washington, DC: Regnery Gateway, 1990.

La Harpe, Jean Francois de. *The Prophecy of Cazotte*. Paris, n.d.

Lefebvre, Georges. *The Coming of the French Revolution*, trans. Robert R. Palmer. Princeton: Princeton University, 1947.

Lichtenberger, Andre. *Le socialisme au XVIII siècle; étude sur les idées socialistes dans le ecrivains francais du XVIII siècle avant la révolution*. Paris: F. Alcan, 1895.

Lichtenberger, Andre. *Le socialisme et la révolution francaise: étude sur les idées socialistes en France, 1789 à 1796*. Paris: F. Alcan, 1899.

Loe, Richard N. *Morelly, Ein Rationalist auf dem Wege zum Sozialismus*. Berlin: Rütten & Loening, 1961.

Mably, Gabriel Bonnet de. *Oeuvres complètes*, 12 vols. Lyon, 1792.

Maistre, Joseph de. *On God and Society*. Washington, DC: Regnery Gateway, 1990.

May, Henry. *The Enlightenment in America*. New York: Oxford University Press, 1976.

McDonald, Joan. *Rousseau and the French Revolution, 1762–1791*. (n.p., 1965).

McManners, John. *The French Revolution and the Church*. Westport: Greenwood Press, 1982.

Miller, James. *Rousseau: Dreamer of Democracy*. New Haven: Yale University Press, 1984.

Montaigne, Michael Eyquem de. *Essays of Montaigne*, trans. E. J. Trechmann. New York: Oxford University Press, n.d.

Morelly. *Code de la nature*. Paris: Raymond Clavrenil, 1950.

Nisbet, Robert A. "The Social Impact of the Revolution," *America's Continuing Revolution: An Act of Conservation*. Washington, D.C.: American Enterprise Institute, 1975.

Ozouf, Mona. "La Revolution francaise et l' idée de l' homme noveau," *The French Revolution and the Creation of Modern Political Culture*, 2 vols., ed. Colin Lucas. New York: Oxford University Press, 1988.

Palmer, Robert R. *The Age of Democratic Revolution: A Political History of Europe and America, 1760–1888*, 2 vols. Princeton: University of Princeton Press, 1959.

Palmer, Robert R. *The World of the French Revolution*. New York: Harper & Row, 1971.

Payne, Stanley G. *The Franco Regime, 1936–1975*. Madison: University of Wisconsin Press, 1987.

Pole, J. R. *The Pursuit of Equality in American History*. Berkeley: University of California Press, 1978.

Robbins, Caroline. *The 18th-Century Commonwealthman*. Cambridge: Harvard University Press, 1959.

Romain, Jules. *Les hommes de bonne Volonté*, n.d.

Rose, R. B. *Gracchus Babeuf: The First Revolutionary Communist*. Stanford: Stanford University Press, 1978.

Rousseau, Jean-Jacques. *Du Contrat social: ou, Principles du droit politique*. Paris: Garnier Frères, 1962.

Sanchez, José M. *The Spanish Civil War as a Religious Tragedy*. Notre Dame: University of Notre Dame Press, 1987.

Sieyè, Abbé. *Qu' est-ce que la tiers état?*, ed. Edme. Champion. Paris: Société d' histoire de la révolution francaise, 1888.

Smith, Adam. *The Theory of Moral Sentiments*. Edinburgh: J. Hay & Co., 1813.

Soboul, Albert. *The French Revolution, 1787–1799: From the Storming of the Bastille to Napoleon*, trans. Alan Forrest and Colin Jones. New York, 1975.

Solzhenitsyn, Aleksandr I. *The Gulag Archipelago*, 3 vols. New York: Harper & Row, 1967.

Stanlis, Peter J. *Edmund Burke and the Natural Law*. Shreveport: Huntington House, Inc., 1986.

Stanlis, Peter J., ed. *Edmund Burke: Selected Writings and Speeches*. Chicago: Regnery Gateway, 1963.

Sybel, Heinrich von. *History of the French Revolution*, 4 vols. (n.p., 1869).

Taylor, George V. "Noncapitalist Wealth and the Origins of the French Revolution," *American Historical Review*, Vol. 72 (1967).

Thibaudeau, Antoine-Clair. *Mémoires*, 2 vols. Paris, 1824.

Thompson, J. M. *Robespierre*, 2 vols. New York: Oxford University Press, 1935.

Tocqueville, Alexis de. *The Old Regime and the French Revolution*, trans. Stuart Gilbert. Garden City: Doubleday & Co., 1955.

Walzer, Michael. "The King's Trial and the Political Culture of the Revolution," *The French Revolution and the Creation of Modern Political Culture*, 2 vols., ed. Colin Lucas. New York: Oxford University Press, 1988.

White, Andrew Dickson. *Fiat Money Inflation in France*. Washington, D.C.: Cato Institute Press, 1980.

White, Morton Gabriel. *The Philosophy of the American Revolution*. New York: Oxford University Press, 1978.

Wolfe, Bertram D. *Three Who Made a Revolution*, 2 vols. New York: Dial Press, 1948.

Wood, Gordon S. "Revolution and the Political Integration of the Enslaved and Disenfranchised," *America's Continuing Revolution: An Act of Conservation*. Washington, D.C.: American Enterprise Institute, 1975.

Wood, Gordon S. *The Creation of the American Republic, 1776–1787*. Chapel Hill: University of North Carolina Press, 1969.

Wright, Gordon. *France in Modern Times: From the Enlightenment to the Present*. Chicago: Rand McNally College Publishing Co., 1974.

Zavala, Silvio. "The Frontiers of Hispanic America," *The Frontier in Perspective*, eds. Walker D. Wyman and Clifton B. Kroeber. Madison: University of Wisconsin Press, 1965.

175

INDEX